CISSP

CYBERSECURITY OPERATIONS
AND INCIDENT RESPONSE

DIGITAL FORENSICS WITH EXPLOITATION
FRAMEWORKS & VULNERABILITY SCANS

RICHIE MILLER

Disclaimer

Every effort was made to produce this book as truthful as possible, but no warranty is implied. The author shall have neither liability nor responsibility to any person or entity concerning any loss or damages ascending from the information contained in this book. The information in the following pages are broadly considered to be truthful and accurate of facts, and such any negligence, use or misuse of the information in question by the reader will render any resulting actions solely under their purview.

Table of Contents

Introduction

IT Security jobs are on the rise! Small, medium or large size companies are always on the look out to get on board bright individuals to provide their services for Business as Usual (BAU) tasks or deploying new as well as on-going company projects. Most of these jobs requiring you to be on site but since 2020, companies are willing to negotiate with you if you want to work from home (WFH). Yet, to pass the Job interview, you must have experience. Still, if you think about it, all current IT security professionals at some point had no experience whatsoever. The question is; how did they get the job with no experience? Well, the answer is simpler then you think. All you have to do is convince the Hiring Manager that you are keen to learn and adopt new technologies and you have willingness to continuously research on the latest upcoming methods and techniques revolving around IT security. Here is where this book comes into the picture. Why? Well, if you want to become an IT Security professional, this book is for you! If you are studying for CompTIA Security+ or CISSP, this book will help you pass your exam. Passing security exams isn't easy. In fact, due to the raising security beaches around the World, both above mentioned exams are becoming more and more difficult to pass. Whether you want to become an Infrastructure Engineer, IT Security Analyst or any other Cybersecurity Professional, this book (as well as the other books in this series) will certainly help you get there! But, what knowledge are you going to gain from this book? Well, let me share with you briefly the agenda of this book. First, you are going to discover what are the most important steps for cyber security operations and incident response, specifically revolving around assessing organizational security. We'll also talk about network reconnaissance and discovery and the various things we can use to accomplish those tasks. Next, we are going to cover file manipulation and the tools we use to do that along with shell and scripting environments. We'll talk about packet capture and replay, data forensics with exploitation frameworks, password crackers, and data sanitization. After that, we'll be covering Appropriate Data Sources to Support an Incident, vulnerability scans and the output, SIEM and SIEM dashboards. We'll also talk about log files and how they can support an investigation or data analysis, trying to figure out what happened, where, when, why and how. Next, you will discover how to use syslog, rsyslog, syslog-ng, journal control and nxlog. We'll also talk about retention for email, audit logs, bandwidth monitors, metadata, and how it changes for different types of files. After that, you will learn how to use NetFlow, sFlow, protocol analyzers and outputs. Moving on, you will discover how to implement Mitigation Techniques to Secure an Environment, how to reconfigure endpoint security solutions, application whitelisting and blacklisting, along with quarantining. We'll also going to cover configuration changes, firewall rules, MDM, or mobile device management, and data loss prevention or DLP. Next you will learn about content filters, revoking and updating certificates, the concepts of isolation, containment, and segmentation and how those can help us secure the environment, along with secure orchestration, automation, and response, or SOAR systems, and runbooks and playbooks specifically. Next we will cover the Key Aspects of Digital Forensics, documentation and evidence gathering in general and why it's very important. We'll also going to talk about acquisition and what we should go after first and why. We'll also cover integrity and a few methods we can use to prove that the data we've collected has not been tampered with, along with preservation, ediscovery and what that means and how it applies to an investigation of data recovery, including the concept of nonrepudiation so the party in question can't deny ownership or a specific action. You are also going to learn about strategic intelligence and counterintelligence along with on-prem versus cloud and some of the challenges and nuances to where that data resides, some things around data sovereignty and applicable laws, depending upon where it's located in the country or in the world if we're doing global business. If you are ready to get on this journey, let's first cover vulnerability scans and the outputs, as well as what we can do with those outputs!

Chapter 1 Data Sources to Support an Incident

In this chapter, we'll be covering an Appropriate Data Sources to Support an Incident. We'll be talking about vulnerability scans and the output, what we do with those outputs. We'll talk about SIEM and SIEM dashboards. We'll talk about log files and how they can support an investigation or data analysis, trying to figure out what happened, where, when, why and how. We'll talk about syslog, rsyslog, and syslog-ng or next generation. We'll talk about the differences there. We'll also talk about something called journal control or journalctl, nxlog. We'll talk about retention for basic things like email, audit logs. Then we'll talk about bandwidth monitors, metadata, and how it changes for different types of files. We'll talk about NetFlow and sFlow, the differences between the two, and then a little bit about protocol analyzers and outputs. When we're talking about accessing all of these different types of data, interpreting assessment results, understanding what's going on, the amount of data that's being created is increasing exponentially, so the amount of sensors, telemetry data. In this chapter, we'll be talking about Implementing Mitigation Techniques to Secure an Environment. We'll be talking about reconfiguring endpoint security solutions, talking about application whitelisting and blacklisting, how that can help us, along with quarantining. We'll talk about configuration changes, and that deals with firewall rules, MDM, or mobile device management, data loss prevention, or DLP. We'll talk about content filters and also revoking and updating certificates. We'll also talk about the concepts of isolation, containment, and segmentation and how those can help us secure the environment, along with secure orchestration, automation, and response, or SOAR systems, and runbooks and playbooks specifically.

In this chapter we'll be talking about Understanding the Key Aspects of Digital Forensics. We'll talk about documentation and evidence in general and why it's Very important to make sure things are documented properly. We'll talk about acquisition and some things around what we should go after first and why, some of the gotchas if we don't follow those procedures. We'll talk about integrity and a few methods we can use to prove that the data we've collected has not been tampered with. We'll talk about preservation along the same lines. We'll talk about ediscovery and what that means and how it applies to an investigation, along with data recovery, and then a similar concept of nonrepudiation so the party in question can't deny ownership or specific action. And then we'll talk about strategic intelligence and counterintelligence along with on-prem versus cloud and some of the challenges and nuances to where that data resides, some things around data sovereignty, applicable laws, depending upon where it's located in the country or in the world if we're doing global business.

Chapter 2 How to Assess Organizational Security

In this chapter, we'll be talking about operations and incident response specifically around assessing organizational security. We'll be talking about network reconnaissance and discovery and the various things we can use to accomplish those tasks. We'll be talking about file manipulation and the tools we use to do that along with shell and scripting environments. We'll talk about packet capture and replay. We'll also talk about data forensics along with exploitation frameworks, password crackers, and then wrap up with data sanitization. To start off, let's talk about traceroute or tracert. It's a network tool to test connectivity between the host and the target. What it does is allow us to see hops along the way. And when I say hop, meaning we're crossing a router. We're going from one network to another. It allows us to see the hops along the way and then the associated latency with each hop. As an example, when I do a traceroute, what I see is the hop count, and it will go from 1 to whatever number. Typically, it tops out at 30. And then it will show me the round-trip time or the RTT for those three attempts. All along the way, I will see an output that shows me those individual hops and the individual round-trip time or the latency for each of those hops. Whether you're troubleshooting network performance or you're just trying to determine what's in between you and your target, it can show you where things might be a bottleneck, where there may be some type of firewall rule, where things are not necessarily reachable. Just because you've see no response or an asterisk doesn't necessarily mean that there's an issue. It just means that that specific hop is not replying back. It can still pass that traffic through to the destination.

nslookup/dig
Next we have nslookup or the Linux equivalent called dig. It's a DNS troubleshooting tool for Windows or Linux and also for Mac operating systems. They can provide a wide range of information on DNS and associated troubleshooting. Nslookup can be used on Windows and Linux systems; whereas, dig is a Linux and Mac-only command. I can do a number of different things. Like I can say set type=mx, and I'm saying, give me DNS information, and I'm going to put in the domain name of Google. But I'm setting the type to mx, so give me only the mail exchanger records. It returns back when I'm using for DNS. And then it also provides a priority number of which ones that should try first. In this particular instance, it's hosted at google.com. Nslookup and dig can both provide a wealth of information. They can

potentially do zone transfers. You can look at all of the DNS information if that specific domain allows those types of lookups. Then to put in the perspective of a forensic examination, these things come in handy when we're doing reconnaissance, trying to figure out where things are going, where they're coming from, perhaps a piece of malware we're trying to track back and get information on the systems that it's touching or reaching out to. All of these different tools, but they help to give us information when we're conducting our investigations or doing reconnaissance.

ipconfig/ifconfig

The next command line told you're probably familiar with is ipconfig or ifonfig. So on the Windows side, that would be ipconfig. On the Linux or Mac side, that would be ifconfig. If I type in ifconfig, you'll see the interfaces, like eth0. Some information about its IP address, its net mask or subnet mask, the broadcast IP address, also its TCP/IP version 6 address. Also, some information about the number of packets received, any errors, and then it's also showing the loopback address. These commands are great for getting your own information as far as IP address, whether it be IPv4 or IPv6. Also it can show you your configured DNS address and, on a Window system, perhaps your WINS Server, not much in use any more. But the point being it can show all the associated information with that specific interface. If you have multiple interfaces, you can bring up information about each.

nmap and nmap demo
Nmap is an open source network scanner and it can discover hosts, it can look at services, it can detect operating systems, vulnerabilities. It's very extensible through the use of the nmap scripting engine, or NSE, and some typical uses for nmap would be device auditing, whether it be host for firewall enumeration, and it can detect vulnerabilities in operating systems, network devices, applications, also, rogue machine detection to identify machines that should not be on a specific network or network inventory. It's a penetration testers tool and network troubleshooting tool that can be used by the good guys, and it's also used very much by the bad guys. Nmap is a very extensible, very powerful program, the full use of which is beyond the scope of the book, but let's just suffice it to say that is a very robust network scanning tool, host enumeration detecting flaws or vulnerabilities that we can then further penetration test, either with scripts that can add or increase the functionality or brute force techniques, or even using other tools that nmap can be a part of, we can use in conjunction with other things. As part of the

toolbox that we would use for penetration testing and, of course, what hackers would also use for their malicious activities. We can do threat detections, we can incorporate scripts through the nmap scripting engine, I can target a specific host, or a subnet, or an entire network. With all of these switches and all of these parameters available to you, just understand that these types of tools should be used in a controlled environment. I would not recommend that you take this into your workplace and start scanning a production environment, that could lead to some bad juju. Your teammates or security folks in other areas perhaps, depending on how big your company is, could see that there are some port scans going on, it could raise some red flags, and then if by some chance it to take down production for some reason, causes congestion on our network, or something bad happens in any way, shape or form, you don't want to be responsible for that. These types of things, should be used in a controlled environment, and then as you develop your penetration testing skills, you can then start using it more in a production environment or in a pen testing engagement if, in fact, you know that's what you're doing at the moment, but just keep that in mind. Keep the usage of these tools to a minimum or in a sandbox environment, at least, until you have proper sign off from the powers that be so that if something does happen, everybody is on board, everyone knows what's happening.

Ping and Pathping

Let's take a look at a few command utilities for network troubleshooting, some things that you should keep in mind, definitely add to your tool bag if you're not already familiar. The first will be ping and pathping. These are two troubleshooting tools, command line tools, for both Windows and Linux., pathping is just for Windows. But ping is pretty much ubiquitous, and that's for Windows or Linux. And that's a network troubleshooting tool to test network connectivity by sending what's called ICMP packets to a host. Pathping does something very similar, but it also combines the features of ping and traceroute. Next would be hping, and hping is a packet crafting tool that can be used to generate traffic, craft packets (spoofed IP addresses, ICMP floods). Then also Netstat. Netstat displays network statistics about TCP and UDP connections, various ports, routing tables, and also protocol statistics. If we look at ping or pathping, again, a tool to test network connectivity. And ping stands for packet internetwork groper, and it sends ICMP packets or internet control message protocol packets to a host to test connectivity. ICMP, internet control message protocol, and what it does is send an echo, and then it expects back a request. You can think of it as like a sonar, like a submarine that sends out a ping. It goes out and hits an object under the water, and it bounces back, and they can tell that that object is there. A very similar concept here.

hping

Hping, which is hping3 is a package generation tool that can craft packets, it can spoof packets, and configure any number of options as needed. We can do SYN attacks, we can flood the network, we can spoof IP addresses, so a lot of functionality here to test firewall collectivity, to test IDS or IPS systems, also for training with Wireshark to craft specific types of packets We can adjust source ports, destination ports, spoof IP addresses. We can simulate in a very small way a denial-of-service attack on a Linux host. I will be sending packets to another Windows host on my network. I have my Linux host, and then I have a Windows host. On the Linux machine if I issue the command hping3, which is going to invoke that hping program. I'm going to put hping3 -S, which is issuing a SYN packet. I give it the destination address, what port I want it to go over, port 135 in this case, and then I'm going to flood the network. I'm telling it, send it as fast as possible.

```
                                                          kali@kali: ~
File  Edit  View  Search  Terminal  Help
root@kali:/home/kali# hping3 -S 192.168.10.129 -p 135 --flood
HPING 192.168.10.129 (eth0 192.168.10.129): S set, 40 headers + 0 data bytes
hping in flood mode, no replies will be shown
```

If I go ahead and hit Enter, it's telling me it's going to go into flood mode. No replies are going to be shown because this is going so fast. If I flip back over to my Windows host, you see my Ethernet connection went from zero up to maxed out.

I'm receiving about 40MB per second, 40MB per second of throughput. This is just one machine sending to another. Imagine if we had 10 or 20 or 100 different machines all sending packets to a host on the network. Same thing with the CPU. We can see that CPU jumped up from nothing to about 38, 39, 40% of activity. That's one host attacking. If I had three or four of these, I could very quickly overrun that host machine. Just to go back in my Linux machine, if I cancel that out, Ctrl+C, I stop it, go back to Windows, you can see the activity drops, CPU drops, and then the Ethernet connectivity drops as well.

Each ping is a very powerful tool. It allows you to fire up Wireshark, look at different types of packets. You can craft packets in a number of ways and then, of course, use it for malicious purposes as well.

Netstat

The next one is netstat. And netstat is a command-line utility, and it displays, network statistics, hence the name netstat. TCP, UDP connections, also reports. We can even display the routing table and protocol statistics. Netstat is cross-platform. It's used to troubleshoot and provide network and host information. I can just type in from a command prompt netstat, and it will show me the active connections, the protocol, a local address, a foreign address, and then the state. Then, depending upon what flags you put in, it also gives me the process ID or the PID. That can be useful. You could look into a Task Manager on Windows and see what the process ID is and then associate that with the IP address it's accessing. netstat -a displays all connections and listening ports. If we add -b, that will display the executable involved in creating each connection or listening port. That may be helpful in troubleshooting what is making that connection if you're not sure. -f will display the fully qualified domain name or the FQDN, for that foreign address if it's possible or if it can determine that. It's not always available. But if it is, it will display that. And then netstat -r, will display the routing table. This is another tool added to the toolbox when we're doing network troubleshooting, connection troubleshooting.

netcat
The next one is an application called netcat. netcat is a network troubleshooting or a pen testing or a hacking tool, depending upon who's using it, that can read from and write to network connections, either TCP or UDP. And some common use cases would be port scanning, port redirection. It can be used as a port listener. It can even operate as a remote shell, serving web pages, or even transferring files. It's a very powerful program and can be used in conjunction with other tools like Metasploit. You could install this on a remote machine and then open up a listener on that remote machine and then run commands as if you were local on that machine. You could turn on Remote Desktop. You could do a lot of things that could have some malicious implications. A powerful tool, and like the majority of these types of tools, I

recommend highly that you don't do it in a production environment unless you're looking for a new job. But seriously, make sure you do it in a controlled environment. A sandbox is best until you understand what the tools can do because they can kick off a lot of things behind the scenes or a lot of activity that you may or may not be aware of if you're not that well versed with the application. If it's in a production environment, it could certainly pop up on someone's radar. You don't want to draw unnecessary attention or take out an application or cause some type of production issue. Here's just a quick screenshot of netcat. It's included with Kali Linux. Not all distributions of Linux have it.

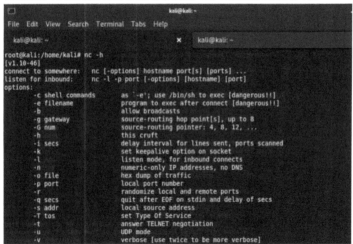

You may need to download and then install. With most of these applications, if you do just a -help or double dash and then the word help, you'll get the actual commands that are available to you. Some of them are very basic. Some of them are very complex. Then netcat, like most of these tools, has extensibility and can be used in conjunction with other applications, Metasploit being one of them. Just be careful with them, but definitely understand what they can do. For a deeper dive, I would definitely recommend some of the other books that go into these in a lot more detail. But for our purposes here, just understand what the application is. Its main use cases would be network troubleshooting, pen testing. Hacking, is one of those. But it's a great pen testing tool and allows us to operate in a listening mode or remote shell mode.

IP Scanners
An IP scanner, as the name implies, scans the network, a range of IP addresses. It can discover hosts. It can test for open ports, troubleshoot connectivity. Some of these things we've already talked about can be certainly identified as IP scanners. Then you can have scaled-down applications that just do the IP scanning part. They don't do a lot of the other enhancements, the remote shells, the remote scripting - all those types of things. Some just identify IP addresses, what ports are available. A few to be aware of, Solarwinds being one, PRTG, AngryIP Scanner, Free IP Scanner, and Nmap as we talked about

previously. All of these things have IP scanning capabilities. Some are more full-featured than others. Some are free, some are paid applications. Everyone has their preference or their favorite. But just make sure you familiarize yourself with the functionality and be sure to add that capability to your toolbelt.

ARP

Another tool and concept to be aware of is arp, and that stands for address resolution protocol, originally developed in 1982. It's been around for a long time by RFC 826, and it resolves an IP address to a MAC address. A link-layer protocol, so it does not route. Arp stays within the local network. But an IP address is a layer 3, if you recall the OSI Model, to a MAC address, which is layer 2. There's also a thing called reverse ARP. That will derive an IP address from a MAC address. And then we talked previously about ARP spoofing. And that is where a malicious user can intercept and reply to ARP requests, also known as ARP cache poisoning so they can put malicious or fictitious information into the ARP cache and either block connectivity or have connectivity go to an improper host.

Route

The next command is route, and route is used to view and manipulate the IP routing table on either

Windows or Linux machines. And when I say Linux, we can general refer to macOS as well. If I just do a route print, it will show me the routing table. And you can see the destination, the net mask, the gateway, the interface, and then the metric. We can also view the routing table if we do a netstat -r. So there are two ways to get to the same information.

Curl and Curl Demo
Next we have a pretty neat command, and that's called curl. And curl can transfer data to or from a server using one of various protocols. But the takeaway here is that it allows us to transfer files, to get web pages, to download things from the internet, as an example, without having to do it from a web page. Web pages are great. They're GUI. They're easy to deal with from a human's perspective. But if we want to script something, we can't script web activity very well. You can't script moving a mouse, clicking on a link. Within curl, you can do the same actions, but from a command line, and allow you to download a file, upload a file, transfer in some form or fashion using it programmatically via scripts. Let's do a quick demo and take a look at using curl to download a file via FTP. So here we are back at our Kali Linux terminal. If I type curl -h, then it gives me the options of what I can do.

```
                              kali@kali:~                        _ □ x
File  Edit  View  Search  Terminal  Help
root@kali:/home/kali# curl -h
Usage: curl [options...] <url>
 -d, --data <data>      HTTP POST data
 -f, --fail             Fail silently (no output at all) on HTTP errors
 -h, --help <category>  Get help for commands
 -i, --include          Include protocol response headers in the output
 -o, --output <file>    Write to file instead of stdout
 -O, --remote-name      Write output to a file named as the remote file
 -s, --silent           Silent mode
 -T, --upload-file <file> Transfer local FILE to destination
 -u, --user <user:password> Server user and password
 -A, --user-agent <name> Send User-Agent <name> to server
 -v, --verbose          Make the operation more talkative
 -V, --version          Show version number and quit

This is not the full help, this menu is stripped into categories.
Use "--help category" to get an overview of all categories.
For all options use the manual or "--help all".
root@kali:/home/kali#
```

I'll go out to a test website that allows me just to test download speeds, and I'll use the -o to give the same name as the one I'm downloading. In this case, speedtest.tele2.net, and we want to download just the sample 10MB file. By using the standard switches, it shows me the download. You can see we use curl to download the file via FTP.

```
                              kali@kali:~                        _ □ x
File  Edit  View  Search  Terminal  Help
root@kali:/home/kali# curl -O ftp://speedtest.tele2.net/10MB.zip
  % Total    % Received % Xferd  Average Speed   Time    Time     Time  Current
                                 Dload  Upload   Total   Spent    Left  Speed
100 10.0M  100 10.0M    0     0  1178k      0  0:00:08  0:00:08 --:--:-- 2195k
root@kali:/home/kali#
```

If I change that to a dash pound, you then see it changed the output from a standard download to I'm getting a progress bar. It will show me the progress of the file. And then once that's downloaded, it will finish.

It allows us to do some things that we would typically do via an FTP program or accessing something via the web. We can do that programmatically and incorporate those things into our scripts.

The Harvester

The next one up is another penetration testing tool, and that's called the Harvester. The Harvester is a tool for gathering email accounts and subdomain names from public sources. A quick screenshot showing you the splash page when you fire up the application. I'm going to be running this from Kali Linux.

The Harvester has a number of different options. Two I just want to call your attention to. Number 1 is -d, and that is the domain name to search or the company name. And then -b would be your data source or where you want to look from. And you can pick one source or you can pick all of them. I have a number of things that I can search through, and you can see the list here. If you did a -b and then chose it would search through all of those different sources. Depending upon what of these that you're scanning, you may return a number of records or not much. It just depends on how much information is publicly accessible. But nevertheless, a great tool for information gathering as you work through your initial reconnaissance and pen testing activities. And it can also be used for malicious activities as well because any tool that can be used for good, it can also be used for malicious purposes as well.

Sn1per

The next one up is sn1per and it's another pen testing tool. This one is an automated penetration testing tool and it can operate in stealth mode, it can do a full scan, it can do port scans only, it can scan individual hosts or entire networks, much like some of these other tools that we've talked about, and it's also very extensible with scripting. It can use scripting via nmap or MetaSploit and others, along with creating reports, including screenshots of websites that it goes out and crawls. It also leverages several other testing and exploit tools, MetaSploit being one, nmap, Slack, Shodan, it integrates with these different tools, and it can also brute force all open services on a target system, so a pretty powerful tool, definitely one to take a look at, especially considering a lot of this can be automated, not a lot of heavy lifting. You point it at something, kickoff some commands, and then off it goes. Let's go ahead and take a quick look at installing Sn1per and then a basic scan. As you can see here from the GitHub page, there is a download location, What I would do is go to my Kali Linux terminal, put in that download location. If I jump into a terminal session and then I put in the git clone and then the HTTPS address, write the GitHub address of that Sn1per installation, from there, I would do a sudo command to get to an elevated prompt and then run a bash script that does the install of the Sn1per application, so bash install.sh and that would run me through the actual installation.

So on my machine, it's about a 7 to 8 minutes installation. On yours, it may be longer, maybe shorter, but rather than have you sit through everything, we'll zip through the installation real quick. Then once it completes, you'll see that it gives us the message saying all done. And then to run the application, you would type Sn1per from your terminal and then, you'll have to give it a target, and then if you have any options that you want it to run, you would put those in as well. As you can see here from the command prompt, if I type sniper -h, it gives me the help file and shows me all the different configuration commands that I can use with the application.

I could run in normal mode just by saying sniper -t and then giving it a target, and then there is a number of other things, a lot of extensibility here. You could go into stealth mode, discover mode, you could run web only, Port 80, Port 443, but at a minimum, it goes in and scans the entire website, all the URLs, all the subdomains, and it puts all of those things into files you can later analyze or look at in more detail, it puts it into what's called a loot folder, and then from there, you can do additional vulnerability testing, penetration testing. A lot of information beyond the scope of this book here to dig into with any detail, but definitely be aware that it's a powerful program for pen testing. Based upon what options you choose when you initiate your scan, some of these things will be skipped, which it goes through a number of different things. It will numerate ports, it will do port scans, it will check the web application firewall if there is one, see if there is any vulnerabilities there, it goes through a number of different nmap scripts, and on and on. I'm just going to zip through this and you can just see there is a lot of information that it scans through, all of the subpages, and it puts all of these things into a file You can go back and analyze it at a later date so that you could go back and do further penetration testing. As you develop pen testing skills, this is a very powerful tool and something you'd want to use quite a bit for doing reconnaissance, but just to play around with, I'm saying, make sure you understand what you're doing before you point it into anything into production. But at the end, and this took about 20 minutes give or take, a scan will complete and then it saves all of those things into a workspace file that's on your machine that you could go back and there is probably 15 or 20 different folders and files that have all the information that was the outputs from these scans that you can then ingest into other applications or read through for further analysis.

Chapter 3 File Manipulation & Packet Captures

Scanless

Another tool that you should be aware of is one called scanless. And scanless is a port scanner that leverages online port scanning services to anonymize scanning a target system. You're not doing it from your own system. You're telling the application to go out and hit a number of websites and have port scans issued from those websites. You can see here, here are the ones that it can go out and target, so Hackertarget, Ipfingerprints, Spiderip, Standingtech. You can read through the rest. But you can initiate these scans from these web-based points of origin. You anonymize where it's coming from. They can't tell it's coming from a specific system. If I want to install scanless on my system, I did a quick Google search and found a link for scanless.

Download scanless:

scanless 1.0.4 can be checked out from it's GIT repository here.

Here it's saying 1.0.4., when I go over to Git's website, it's version 2.1.5 is the latest as of this time. It shows me the install, which is pip install scanless.

scanless	v2.1.5	last month
.gitignore	Update .gitignore	4 years ago
Dockerfile	Dockerfile added	2 years ago
README.md	v2.1.4, minor fix to web request func	2 months ago
UNLICENSE	initial commit	4 years ago
setup.py	v2.1.5	last month

From a terminal session, I'll go ahead and issue that command. It then downloads and installs scanless on my system.

It will upack it, install, and then I'm good to go. So from there, I can do a scanless -h as I talked about before. It gives me the arguments. I can see the current version. I can pick a target, with no additional switches. I can then run the same command again with a -a, which will give me all of the online scanners. And it will run through all of those. It might take a minute or two. And each of the online services might give me slightly different results. Some scan for more ports than others, so you don't get exactly the same results from each. But what it does do, is anonymize those scans.

DNSenum

The next one that I want to mention is one called DNSenum for enumerate. DNSenum is a command line tool, and I just have a screenshot here showing you the help file and some of the switches that you can use.

```
                                                  kali@kali ~
File  Edit  View  Search  Terminal  Help
kali@kali:~$ dnsenum -h
dnsenum VERSION:1.2.6
Usage: dnsenum [Options] <domain>
[Options]:
Note: If no -f tag supplied will default to /usr/share/dnsenum/dns.txt or
the dns.txt file in the same directory as dnsenum.pl
GENERAL OPTIONS:
  --dnsserver    <server>
                          Use this DNS server for A, NS and MX queries.
  --enum                  Shortcut option equivalent to --threads 5 -s 15 -w.
  -h, --help              Print this help message.
  --noreverse             Skip the reverse lookup operations.
  --nocolor               Disable ANSIColor output.
  --private               Show and save private ips at the end of the file domain_ips.txt.
  --subfile <file>        Write all valid subdomains to this file.
  -t, --timeout <value>   The tcp and udp timeout values in seconds (default: 10s).
  --threads <value>       The number of threads that will perform different queries.
  -v, --verbose           Be verbose: show all the progress and all the error messages.
GOOGLE SCRAPING OPTIONS:
  -p, --pages <value>     The number of google search pages to process when scraping names,
                          the default is 5 pages, the -s switch must be specified.
  -s, --scrap <value>     The maximum number of subdomains that will be scraped from Google (default 15).
BRUTE FORCE OPTIONS:
  -f, --file <file>       Read subdomains from this file to perform brute force. (Takes priority over default dns.txt)
```

If I go in and just scrape down through here, I can get a lot of information about a specific website, its zones and subzones. I can tell it where to scrape from, reverse lookup options or output options. If I just do a DNSenum -v for verbose and then I put in the website, it shows me the web servers, any name servers, mail exchangers. It can go out and, as the name implies, enumerate DNS entries and DNS information about a specific website.

Nessus and Cuckoo

Nessus is a commercial vulnerability scanner. There's three different versions. There's a professional version, a cloud version, and then a free version. The professional version you could install local or have it on your system.

A cloud version, as the name implies, runs in the cloud as a service. The free version will be good for very small environments or for educational use. That's limited to scanning 16 IP addresses. Very limited use, but still gives you a good opportunity to learn about the product. The nice thing about Nessus is it's a very mature product, and it has many built-in templates and scans for common threats, misconfigurations. Definitely one to familiarize yourself with if your organization is looking for a commercial vulnerability scanner. Next, let's talk about something called Cuckoo. Cuckoo is an automated malware analysis platform, and it runs in a sandboxed environment. You would want to run it in the virtualized environment with a sandbox set up so that you can download malware and let that malware execute in that sandbox to see what it does.

More specifically, Cuckoo, it's an open source automated malware analysis tool, and it's designed to be run in an isolated lab environment. It can analyze, trace, and document a piece of malware's actions. It can do tracing of API calls. It can analyze memory and network traffic. It's a great tool to have in a controlled environment. As an example, here we have a Cuckoo host machine. That's going to do our guest analysis management, traffic dumps, and reporting. That's going to be attached, to an isolated network, a virtual isolated network. It's important that we run this thing in a sandboxed environment so that when we do download malware and we run that malware, it doesn't have the potential to escape out onto our production environment. That would be very bad. That's what we call an RGE or a resume-generating event. Isolated network, and in this small example, we have three virtual machines. We have a Windows machine, a Linux machine, and an OSX machine, your virtual environment may be a lot larger, or you may have a different mix of hosts, but you get the idea. Then from there, you could have that host machine go out to the internet you can see if it is, in fact, pulling things down from some command and control server. Or you could have it point to a sinkhole so it goes here. And then you can download this from cuckoosandbox.org and try it out in your own environment.

File Manipulation

Next, I just want to talk about a few file manipulation commands that you can use from a command line. The first would be head. The head command would print the first x number of lines of a file, so the default would be 10. However, that's configurable. Tail is the opposite of that. That prints the last x number of lines of a file. The default is 10. We have the command cat, which would create, display, and also concatenate files or combine files together. And then we have grep. Grep searches plain-text data for lines that match a regular expression. It means globally search for a regular expression and then print matching lines. That's where the term grep comes from, but it's a very, very powerful tool. If you're not already familiar with grep and regular expressions, I definitely recommend you dig into that and learn all about that and add that skillset to your toolbox. From the command line, it's very, very powerful. Next, we have chmod or change permissions on files and folders. We can change permissions on files and folders, again from the command line. And then lastly, logger. Logger is going to create entries in a system log. It provides the shell command interface to the syslog system-log chapter. Back in my Kali Linux terminal, I have a text file here, just as an example, and, inside the file, just some random text. If I go into the terminal and issue a head command, and I can just drag this file in there.

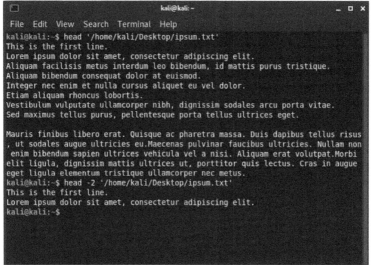

That will give me the path directly to it. And I can just hit Enter. That's going to give me the first 10 lines of that file. If I want to just say the first one line or, say, first two lines, I could just hit a -2, and it would give me just the first two lines of that file. Conversely, if I type tail, same thing, and let's say do the last two lines of the file and drop that off, there's a space and then the very last line of the file. And if I open it up in the regular text editor, you can see the first few lines of the file and then, down at the bottom, the last line of the file. It makes it easy to work with very large files from the command line, getting to the beginnings or the ends of files. Same type of thing with the cat demand. If I just did a cat and then help, it gives me the flags that I can use. And if I just type in cat and then, let's say, for instance, a n for line number, again drop that file into the terminal window and hit Enter, it shows me then the same file, but it numbers every single line.

```
                                 kali@kali: ~                           _ □ ✕

 File  Edit  View  Search  Terminal  Help
 Examples:
   cat f - g  Output f's contents, then standard input, then g's contents.
   cat        Copy standard input to standard output.

 GNU coreutils online help: <https://www.gnu.org/software/coreutils/>
 Full documentation <https://www.gnu.org/software/coreutils/cat>
 or available locally via: info '(coreutils) cat invocation'
 kali@kali:~$ cat -n '/home/kali/Desktop/ipsum.txt'
      1  This is the first line.
      2  Lorem ipsum dolor sit amet, consectetur adipiscing elit.
      3  Aliquam facilisis metus interdum leo bibendum, id mattis purus tristique

      4  Aliquam bibendum consequat dolor at euismod.
      5  Integer nec enim et nulla cursus aliquet eu vel dolor.
      6  Etiam aliquam rhoncus lobortis.
      7  Vestibulum vulputate ullamcorper nibh, dignissim sodales arcu porta vita
 e.
      8  Sed maximus tellus purus, pellentesque porta tellus ultrices eget.
      9
     10  Mauris finibus libero erat. Quisque ac pharetra massa. Duis dapibus tell
 us risus, ut sodales augue ultricies eu.Maecenas pulvinar faucibus ultricies. Nu
 llam non enim bibendum sapien ultrices vehicula vel a nisi. Aliquam erat volutpa
 t.Morbi elit ligula, dignissim mattis ultrices ut, porttitor quis lectus. Cras i
 n augue eget ligula elementum tristique ullamcorper nec metus.
```

This may or may not be useful for you depending upon what environment you like to work in. But definitely understand the uses of them, the flags associated with them, and how they can be used to in scripting or manipulating files from the command line.

Shell and Script Environments (SSH, PowerShell, Python and OpenSSL)

Just to cover some shell and scripting environments without digging too deeply, making you an expert in any one specific area, but some things you should be aware of for sure are SSH, or Secure Shell. It is a cryptographic network protocol for doing things securely over an insecure network or an unsecured network. We can do things like remote command line execution, remote logins. Next is PowerShell.

41

PowerShell is a command line shell and associated scripting language. It was originally Windows-only, but has since been made open source, so its cross-platform. But without digging into the specifics, PowerShell has a multitude of commands and functions called cmdlets to access elements of the operating system, to do various functions. Next, we have Python, and Python is a cross-platform interpreted programming language. Meaning you need an interpreter with a focus on readability. It's widely regarded as one of the top three programming languages, Java and C or C# being some of the other ones. Then we have OpenSSL, which is a software library for applications that secure communications using an open-source implementation of SSL and TLS. With TLS 1.3 support added in September of 2018, TLS 1.0 has been deprecated, so make sure that's out of your environment if at all possible. But, TLS 1.3 is the current standard.

Packet Capture and TCPDump
As a security analyst, there's a lot of tools that we need in our toolbelt, a lot of various skills that we need to develop to secure our networks and our applications. When it comes to packet capture and replay, we have a security analyst that's attached to the network, and we have a few other hosts on the network. We have some database and some coding.

There's other users on the network. Well, as a security analyst, there's a few different tools that you may use, one of which is tcpdump, which is a command line utility. Another might be Wireshark, which is a GUI implementation. Tcpdump gives you a similar capability as Wireshark, but it's a command line. And then the ability to replay traffic, tcpreplay, and that could be fed into IDS and IPS systems to ramp up traffic to keep it at scale just to give you a bit of an overview of where these things come into play. When we talk about tcpdump, it's a command line packet capture tool to capture and display packets in real time. It can be filtered by IP address, by port, by connection type or protocol. It's a very quick and dirty tool to be able to see what's going on in real time via command line, much like we do within Wireshark, but this is a command line utility. Next is Wireshark. It's a graphical packet capture utility similar to tcpdump and can be used to troubleshoot network issues, to decrypt communications, assuming we have the proper certificates, and then also to eavesdrop on communications either for a legitimate purpose or an illegitimate purpose. Bad actors can use that maliciously. Then tcpreplay is a command line tool for editing and then replaying previously captured packets. It can be used for troubleshooting, for IDS and IPS systems, intrusion detection systems or intrusion prevention systems, for NetFlow systems.

We want to be able to replay that traffic and analyze it in some form or fashion. This is very similar to what we would see in Wireshark. We're capturing packets. It just happens to be displaying in real time in my terminal session. Depending upon what types of tools you like to use, this could be another tool in your toolbelt. Some people prefer command prompt or command line or terminal session. Other folks prefer graphical user interfaces, like Wireshark.

Chapter 4 Forensics & Exploitation Frameworks

When it comes to forensics, there are a lot of nuances within the field. There are different specialties, different areas of expertise. But generally speaking, there are some tools that you should be aware of and some skill sets that you should develop if forensics is, in fact, an area that you want to dig into. Imagine that we have an investigator, and there are a few tools I just want to call your attention. We have the first one being dd, and that's a command line tool to copy and clone disks, partitions, and files. It can be used to erase disks. Some people refer to it as disk destroyer, but it's a very powerful tool, command line tool, built into Linux and allows you to copy, clone and partition files. Next, we have memdump. Memdump can dump either the physical or kernel memory to a file, and it can also be done over the network. You can connect to a machine remotely and do a memory dump to a file and get what's in that system's memory, either physical memory or kernel memory. Next, we have WinHex, and that's a hex editor for examining files, recovering files, searching for specific file types. That can dig into the code underneath of a file or contained within a file to help you look for specific patterns, hidden information, header-type mismatch. And then we have something called FTK Imager, and that stands for Forensic Toolkit, and it's used to acquire disk images and perform analysis for investigations, creating case files. Then we have Autopsy, another forensic toolkit for acquiring disk images and performing analysis and investigations. Two different ways, or two different programs to accomplish the same task. As an example, here we have a screenshot of Autopsy, this is a forensic tool for building cases for investigating systems, gathering evidence.

It allows us to create a case, we can name it, add additional information, we can put in the base directory of where we want to store that information. Then once we start the case, there are a number of things that can be automated as it searches through that system. We can do hash lookups.

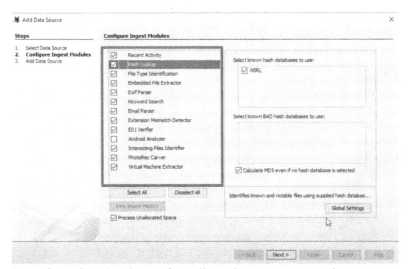

So, if we're looking for illegal images or things we don't necessarily want to have to sift through one by one by one, we can have the application going in and hash all the files on that system and then compare those hashes to a database of known hashes. In other words, if there's a bunch of files that are already known, like child exploitation files as an example, there are large hash databases that have already been compiled by law enforcement that you can subscribe to and then compare those hashes against that. You can very quickly find information without having to sift through each individual file. We can look for file type identification or extension mismatch detector. That's an old school way of trying to hide files. Like you may have a graphics file, but you may change the extension to.doc for a doc file, so that if someone looks at it, they try to click on it, it won't open because it's not associated to the application. By using tools like this, we can very quickly look at the file header and then match it to the file extension. And if those things don't match, it stands out like a sore thumb. It makes it even easier to find those types of files. These types of applications become very powerful. As it does all of these things, it does a lot of it automated. Some of it will be manual process, but some of it is just a matter of you setting things up in the beginning. And then it will go through and analyze that system, build the case file, put everything into proper files and folders, and then something that we've touched on before is the concept of hashing and making sure that hashes match to show that we have two identical files. Well, when we're talking about acquiring forensic images, it's the same process. We have an investigator that would use their forensic toolkit, one of the ones we just talked about, and they would connect it to a target system. They want to acquire an image from a suspect PC to analyze, to investigate. They would typically put a write blocker in between their laptop or their toolkit and the actual target system. That way, it would prevent their forensic toolkit from altering or writing to the target system in any way, shape, or form. It keeps everything pristine. The write blocker would then connect to the target system. Then the forensic toolkit would do its thing. We just saw the screenshot showing some of the capabilities. It would image that system and then write it out to a cloned system. We take all of the data off of the target system and make an immutable copy that's write protected. It may chunk it up into multiple pieces that can be copied out to a CD or a DVD so that it can be then imaged or analyzed over and over again. Then what we can do each time is take a hash of the target system and then a hash of the cloned system. That way, those things match. We know that they are identical, that nothing's changed. That way we can be sure that when we're working off of a cloned system, we're not introducing artifacts or changing data in any way, shape, or form. Those things, as you can imagine, are needed for court, preservation of evidence, chain of custody. All of these things apply when we're dealing with digital evidence, as well as physical evidence, and having a hash value that matches allows us to show when we present that report and say, here's all of the things that we found on that target system. The other side can't come back and say, oh, well, that's not my system. Things have been changed. You added things in there. Well, no, the hash values match. We initially took a hash of the system when we first acquired it, and it exactly matches the hash of our cloned system. Those things go a long way to help strengthen your case. It's a matter of following best practices when we're doing forensic-type work.

Exploitation Frameworks

Exploitation frameworks, and as the name implies, they are there to exploit weaknesses, exploit vulnerabilities in a specific host, or a network, or a system. They are tool sets that can be used offensively or defensively, and they're often used by penetration testers, or pen testers, as well as hackers unfortunately. Popular exploitation frameworks, Metasploit is probably one of the most popular, and it's an open source and commercial, there are both versions available, you can download it for free, and then there's a paid version. It gives you a lot of amazing features and tool sets out of the box, hundreds of different exploits to test, and it's also widely used, by pen testers and also the hacking community. Next is CANVAS. These are just a small list, not an exhaustive one by any stretch and certainly not an endorsement of any one particular piece of software. But CANVAS was a development and pen testing platform originally, and then we have Core Impact, another one, which was designated as the first fully automated pen testing program that's typically used by enterprises and corporate environments primarily due to cost. There's also another one that's called RouterSploit, and as you might guess, that's specifically geared towards routers.

```
rsf (AutoPwn) > set target 192.168.1.254
[+] {'target': '192.168.1.254'}
rsf (AutoPwn) > show options

Target options:

   Name        Current settings      Description
   ----        ----------------      -----------
   target      192.168.1.254         Target address e.g. http://192.168.1.1
   port        80                    Target port


rsf (AutoPwn) > run
[*] Running module...
[-] exploits/multi/misfortune_cookie is not vulnerable
[-] exploits/dlink/dvg_n5402sp_path_traversal is not vulnerable
[-] exploits/dlink/dwr_932_info_disclosure is not vulnerable
[-] exploits/dlink/dir_300_320_615_auth_bypass is not vulnerable
[-] exploits/dlink/dsl_2750b_info_disclosure is not vulnerable
[-] exploits/dlink/dns_3201_3271_rce is not vulnerable
[-] exploits/dlink/dir_645_password_disclosure is not vulnerable
[-] exploits/dlink/dir_300_600_615_info_disclosure is not vulnerable
[-] exploits/dlink/dir_300_600_rce is not vulnerable
[-] exploits/cisco/ucs_manager_rce is not vulnerable
[-] exploits/2wire/gateway_auth_bypass is not vulnerable
[-] exploits/asus/infosvr_backdoor_rce is not vulnerable
[-] exploits/asus/rt_n16_password_disclosure is not vulnerable
[+] exploits/asmax/ar_1004g_password_disclosure is vulnerable
[-] exploits/asmax/ar_804_gu_rce is not vulnerable
[-] exploits/linksys/wap54gv3_rce is not vulnerable
[-] exploits/linksys/1500_2500_rce is not vulnerable
[-] exploits/fortinet/fortigate_os_backdoor is not vulnerable
[-] exploits/technicolor/tc7200_password_disclosure is not vulnerable
```

As you can see here, it runs in very much the same fashion, you can put in a target, an IP address, and you can run a Metasploit-type command set, against this target IP address, and it will run different modules, it'll go through the list, and it will run all of these different types of exploits against that specific router, and it will see where there's a vulnerability or if any exist. And as you can see from the output here, that exploit does exist for a password disclosure, so it says is vulnerable. All the rest in this specific instance is not vulnerable, but it allows you to quickly go through a network and identify all the different routers within a specific subnet or the entire environment, and then run this test against all of those devices, and come back and report and say, hey, here's where we're vulnerable, we're locked down everywhere except, not sure if you knew this, but you're vulnerable here, here, and here. You can very quickly give a report back to management, executive management, or the company that's hiring you to come in if you're a penetration tester, and show them where those vulnerabilities do exist.

Chapter 5 Data Sanitization Tools

Next we have data sanitization tools, and wiping versus deleting, as you may or may not be aware, deleting a file doesn't do much in and of itself. If you delete a file, you're simply marking that file as being able to be overwritten, so the data is still there. There are tons of free tools and commercial tools that can recover that data very easily. If you need to make sure that data is gone and not recoverable, then we need to do something called wiping, Wiping is always going to be better than deleting. Sanitization tools overwrite the data x number of times to ensure that it's unrecoverable, and those number of passes, or that x number of times, is configurable. We'll also talk about SSD disk sanitization. That's going to be different. When we're talking about traditional hard disks, that's a magnetic media, so that's going to be a different method to sanitize than SSDs or the solid state or all-flash drives. With SSDs, each manufacturer typically has a secure erase tool, you'll need to either use that specific tool, or there are also some third-party tools that can work on SSDs as well, so as an example of SSD sanitization. Each manufacturer will have their own specific toolset that is geared toward that specific drive, Samsung, Intel, Corsair, SanDisk, they all make their own different tools. And then there's a third-party tool called Parted Magic, and that includes a sanitization or a secure erase tool as well. As an example, here we have SSD Secure Erase for Samsung drives.

Using the Samsung Magician toolset, we'll create a beautiful drive, either USB or a CD or DVD, and we put that in the machine, and we'll boot into this interface. From here, we just say yes, we want to do a Secure Erase. It'll ask us again, and then within a matter of seconds that drive is securely erased. If we use Parted Magic as an example, it's going to come up first and say, we want to do a secure erase, and it can either be SSDs or it can be NVMe in this case.

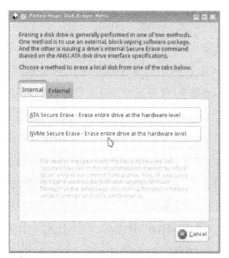

It's going to do a drive-level erase, so Secure Erase issues drive-level command sets to that specific drive and tells it what to do. In this instance, we're going to do a Secure Erase of an NVMe drive. We're going to say, pick the drive from the list. There it is dev/nvme0n1.

It's a Samsung SSD 950 PRO. We're going to say yes, I want to go ahead and erase. From there, it literally takes 2 or 3 seconds, and then it's done. That quickly that drive is securely erased. And it can also generate a log output if you want to review the log settings or review the output, but very quick and much quicker than erasing a magnetic hard disk. When we're talking about data sanitization methods for hard drives, there are a few things or a few standards we should be aware of. There are a couple that I want to call your attention to, and there are others, but these are the main three that you should be familiar with. The first is the DoD 5220.22-M, that's a standard. This is from the Department of Defense, and it is a three-pass write, so it's going to overwrite that data three separate times. Pass 1 writes a zero and then verifies the write, Pass 2 writes a one and then verifies the write, and then Pass 3 writes a random character verifies that write. Once that's complete, that data is not recoverable. The next is RCMP, or the Royal Canadian Mounted Police, an outstanding cybersecurity division. They issue a three-pass write as well. The Communication Security Establishment of Canada, that's what the CSEC stands for. And what we're doing here is writing a one or zero in Pass 1, and then Pass 2 writes the complement of the previously written character, so if the first pass was zeros, then this pass would be a one and vice-versa. Then Pass 3 writes a random character and then verifies that write. Then lastly, something referred to as Secure Erase, and that's a one-pass. That writes a binary one or a zero, very fast, and that's only available for whole-disk sanitization. These other two methods I talked about, they can be used on individual files and folders as well. There are toolsets that you can run within the operating system that will allow you to use those techniques to erase individual files or folders, but with Secure Erase it works only on the whole disk. There are some other ones as well. There's the Peter Gutmann 35-pass, and that was developed back in the mid to late nineties, and back then, 35 passes was thought to be like the most extreme, and that was like super secure. We've found that over time that a subset of that is all you need to have data unrecoverable. It used to be DoD was a seven-pass overwrite, and that was like the most secure. It's going down to three. Same thing with RCMP. They went from a higher level down to three. Then Secure Erase is also acceptable by RCMP as well. That single-pass write has been found to be unrecoverable by pretty much every type of disk recovery software out there. In summary, we talked about network reconnaissance and discovery, along with file manipulation, various shell and script environments. We talked about packet capture and replay, some of the tools that we would use for that, whether they are command-line or GUI based. We also talked about forensics and some of the nuances of acquiring images, making sure that they match, holding up in court. Then we talked about exploitation frameworks, password crackers, data sanitization, and then some demos of various applications.

Chapter 6 How to Apply Policies, Processes and Procedures for Incident Response

In this chapter we'll be talking about applying policies, processes, and procedures for incident response. We'll be talking about incident response plans and process. We'll cover the various testing exercises that you may utilize in your environment. We'll also talk about the various attack frameworks, along with stakeholder management, communication plans, including disaster recovery and business continuity plans. We'll also talk about the continuity of operation planning, along with incident response teams, retention policies, and at the end, we'll put it all together and talk about responding to an incident. But who should read this chapter? Well, we have six main categories. We have computer security staff, people that are implementing this type of stuff day to day; we have computer security program managers, the ones that need to look at things at a little higher level and understand the big risk and also the financial impacts; tech support staff and managers, the folks that make IT run on a day-to-day basis; incident response teams, the ones that are responsible for coming out and handling things when an incident or a breach occurs; system and network administrators, again IT, in general; and then end users, both IT and non-IT. IT security is everyone's responsibility. It's not just for the IT security professional. Everybody is responsible or should be responsible for making sure IT security, information security, cybersecurity, make that a priority. Because, as we know, threats can come both internally and externally. They can come from hackers, organized crime, nation states, but they can also be done internally for things like espionage or to get back at a co-worker or a manager. Then when we look at the actual potential impacts, some things that you should be aware of, drives this home, and the real reasons why you should care, is the fact that companies, both large and small, are constant targets. It makes no difference the industry or the size of the company, not just high-value targets. Smaller victims can play a part in larger attacks. Meaning, you may think to yourself, well, we're a small company of 5, 10, 15 people. We don't have to worry about IT Security as much. Well, that's precisely why you should worry about IT security. The smaller companies that may not have their actual IT network defenses and perimeter defenses as tight and as rigid as some larger companies, they become easy targets. While the information that they possess may not be of a high-value nature to a potential hacker or nation state or what have you, what small company, or your small company, could play a part in a larger attack. You could become part of a botnet or some type of other larger organized or more organized scheme to attack a much larger company or a much larger victim. Don't think just because you're small, you may not play a part in a much bigger attack. Then also such things as loss of data, intellectual property, competitive advantage, or overall consumer confidence. These can all be downstream impacts and fallout from a breach. Then companies can also risk legal action if they're negligent and not properly protected. If there are things that you should be doing but for whatever reason you're not, and then a breach occurs and an incident occurs and consumer data is lost, or personally identifiable information, is leaked, that information, or that fallout could come back to haunt the company in the form of legal action lawsuits, or class action lawsuits. It's very important that we realize that IT security is everyone's responsibility. Everyone should be chipping in. If they see something, say something. Everyone should be playing their part to make sure that their small piece of this larger puzzle is as secure as possible.

Team Models
Let's now talk about the various team models that we should look at developing within our organization. So, we can have a central incident response team, and that means all of our team

members are on site, they're in one central location, and they'll handle all incidents for that company wherever they may be. If we have a global presence, however, that may or may not be feasible. In that case, we would have a distributed incident response team, and that means we have incident response teams perhaps spread out through all of our different organization locations, geographically dispersed, either throughout a specific part of the world or potentially globally. And then we have a coordinating team, and a coordinating team would be centrally located. The coordinating team itself, they would coordinate the efforts of the other teams located throughout the various parts of either the country or throughout the world. No matter which of the last two we choose, whether it's distributed or coordinating, it's very important to understand that all of the different teams, whether they are reporting to a centralized coordinating team and they're advising them what to do, or they're distributed and they're each acting as their own entity, they all need to make sure that they adhere to the same sets of policies so a consistent application of that incident response plan and procedures, are in fact implemented and executed, no matter where that's taking place throughout any of the company's various locations.

Incident Response Process

When talking about the phases of incident response we've covered before, the six main phases, the preparation, detection, analysis, containment, eradication, recovery, and then documentation, or lessons learned. This process is a continuous cycle that's refined over time. None of these things are going to be static. It's a living document; it's a living process. Every time we have a breach or an incident, we're going to learn something from that, and we're going to refine our process. Those lessons learned, once you come to the end of that process, we go through preparation, detection, containment, eradication, we get to the end, the documentation and lessons learned, that helps us identify gaps and increase our preparedness for the next time. It would be nice to say there never will be a next time, but unfortunately, that's not the nature of breaches in today's environment. Most companies have hundreds, if not thousands, of breaches or attempted breaches per year. Some companies have thousands per day. It just depends upon the size of your company, the criticality of the information your company has, or the intellectual property or whatever data that's valuable to a hacker, whoever that hacker or hacking organization may be. Then additional resources are brought on line and into that response team's arsenal. It's not a static environment. It's dynamic, and so as we go through this process and we refine, refine, refine, lessons learned, we identify gaps, we close those gaps. We may need additional resources, additional team members with additional skill sets. Every company's going to be slightly different. Every company houses different information, has different potential targets for a hacker or a hacking organization. There is no one set document that will cover everything. There are certainly a guideline and a best practices, but as you go through this, you will identify specific things that are unique to your organization, and correct or add to that arsenal accordingly.

Preparation
When we're talking about preparation, we have a couple things. We need to make sure that we identify team members. It's very important that we identify what skills we need, how many team members we need. One person can't do all of this. It's too vast. There are too many things to do at once. In the middle of a breach, you're going to have multiple things going on at once, detection and analysis, alerting other people, alerting other teams, coordinating with media, coordinating with executive management, identifying the risk, shutting down ports, protocol, and so on. There's going to be a lot of things that may need to happen concurrently or in tandem in the middle of a breach,

so it's too much for one person to handle, typically. We'll need to identify those team members. We'll need to identify and define roles and responsibilities. It should be clearly defined who does what and in what order, so in the middle of some type of crisis, we have a playbook or a run book we can go by and say, you do this, I'll do this, he's going to take care of that piece for us. Everybody works in concert and attacks the problem as a cohesive unit. It's very important to have that synergy. Then also develop defense-in-depth strategies. These things should be spelled out ahead of time. You shouldn't have just one lock on the door. There are many things that we can do, so that if a hacker breaches one method of defense, there's still another, perhaps two or three more that they have to get through before they can get into our network and into our systems, make it as difficult as possible. That also gives you time to become alerted, it gives you time to remediate before they penetrate all of the defenses and get at your critical systems.

Chapter 7 Detection and Analysis

In the detection and analysis phases, properly trained teams can assist and expedite all phases of the incident and response process. Having that team in place, properly trained, running smooth, that's going to help all phases of that process. A quick assessment can determine the level of impact and also help direct containment and mitigation efforts. That quick initial assessment; is this malware or is it not? Is this a virus? Is this a hacking attempt that came in through maybe a specific port or a protocol? Or they did some type of SQL injection, or they had a USB stick that was infected and brought into our system, or it was infected laptop. By identifying the source and the type of threat, the type of incident we're dealing with here can help quickly identify the level of impact. Is it going to be a nuisance or is it going to be a multimillion dollar event? Are we going to lose customer information? How quickly can we stem that bleeding? That helps direct containment and the mitigation efforts. Also, analysis of event files, log files, from things like intrusion detection systems, firewalls, routers, switches, directory servers. Anything on our network that can be audited or that creates log files that can be parsed and then correlated across different verticals, we can correlate timing from our routers and switches, our firewalls, IDS systems, access to directory servers, or perhaps pieces of critical infrastructure; if we're able to aggregate and then correlate those events across all those devices at one time, it allows us to quickly get a picture of what's happening, and how it's happening. All of those network systems should be brought into play. That helps us determine the true intent of that attack. So, is your company the clear target? In other words, are you the goal, or is someone just probing? They happened to come across one of your systems, and they're just probing just to see what's there. It's the old hacker mantra: Well why'd you climb that mountain? Well, because it was there. Sometimes people just want to probe and see what they can see. They don't have a specific goal, they're not trying to necessarily steal something or destroy something, and they just want to see if they can get in, more or less as a badge of honor, if you will. Alternatively, was your business the actual target, or are you a side door attack to some other company? And as I mentioned earlier, as far as things being a clear target or just probing, was this a true attack or just someone doing an initial network or resource mapping? They want to come in and probe our network and see how things are laid out. What are our routers and switches? Do we have a single namespace? Do we have different IP spaces for different areas, naming conventions? What type of systems do we have? Are we running Linux, Windows or virtualization. By coming in and doing that network mapping, they can get a good idea of what types of systems are on the network. By having that properly trained team, we can identify and say, is this breach? Are we in all hands on deck mode, and we having to go in and start bringing all of our resources to bear to try to confront this and contain it? Or, was this someone coming in initially? Do we catch them in the very beginning hopefully while they're still doing the network scan, trying to go in and see what there is of value. By being able to identify that, it allows us to quickly attack that in the proper fashion, assign resources correctly, and address that threat appropriately.

Stopping the Spread
When it comes to stopping the spread, we want to focus on a couple things. Containing a security incident is going to help mitigate loss. The quicker we can contain that spread or that initial infection of that piece of malware or virus focusing on malware here, the quicker we can contain that, the quicker we can mitigate loss. After containment, then comes eradication. Eradication, it may consist of disabling compromised accounts, taking that machine out of service. Also, potentially wiping that machine and reinstalling from scratch. It all depends

upon that part of the recovery process that deals with backups. If we can verify them as being valid backups, then we may be able to restore that system from that backed up piece of data, that backup tape. If it's not, however, then we may need to completely blow that system away or wipe that system or reimage that system. Also, check it for rootkits and because we want to make sure that that system is not compromised beyond what we initially thought. When it comes to eradication and recovery, we may need to disable affected accounts. We have to identify how that piece of malware was installed. What user account was used? Is it affecting admin accounts? Is our system set up or is our network set up to have admin accounts disabled by default? If there's a service account that it somehow is able to attach itself to and then spread throughout the network using that service account, we have to identify that quickly and disable that account so it can't spread. It just depends upon the nature of that piece of malware. Next, we have to identify what ports and protocols that piece of malware uses. And shut down those ports and protocols or at least monitor them very closely to make sure that malware is not spreading to other systems across that same transport mechanism, that same port or that same protocol. Next, recover from backup, will verify that the backup is, in fact, good. If it's not, then we need to do a fresh install. It's going to depend upon - the nature of that infection. And then something else that's equally as important, if not more important, and we have to do that very quickly, in tandem with the initial infection as we're going through our identification remediation steps, we need to coordinate with other sites and other locations within our company to make sure they're aware of the breach of the infection and so they can start monitoring their systems as well. That if a spread, in fact, does take place or tries to take place, they can mitigate that as quickly as possible. That goes back to what accounts are being used, what ports or protocols. That information should be shared with other sites and with other locations within the company.

Defining Goals and Expected Outcomes
When we're talking about defining goals and expected outcomes, a few things to keep in mind. First off, we need to periodically test the business continuity, cyber and also disaster recovery plans. We have to make sure and verify that the plans are valid, that they cover the required elements that we want to protect, that we're getting all the critical infrastructure, critical applications and all the critical business functions, and that the plan can be executed when the time comes. Doesn't do us much good to have a very grandiose plan, and we think it

might work, but if it doesn't achieve the expected outcome or if it's not even an executable plan, it doesn't do us much good. Many companies have business continuity plans that they've written down, they sound great on paper, but they've never executed them, never tested them. It's important that we do that. Next, we want to make sure we have buy-in from senior management. We must have executive approval, and this should be disseminated, if possible, organization wide so that everyone is aware of what the plans are. We need to make sure that people who are involved with this process know that they're involved with the process and are able to complete and are competent in the roles that they're assigned. Buy-in from executive management is critical in this regard, and then, if possible, it's going to depend on corporate culture, the size of the organization, but if possible, these plans should be disseminated company wide so that everyone is on the same page. Next, we should have post testing review. After we test our plans, we need to identify what's changed, if anything, because as we test our plan, we might identify, we didn't think of this, or, we thought we had this in place, but it's no longer valid, we can remove that. If anything's changed, we need to document, we need to correct any gaps, and then compare our goals and expected outcomes. We thought we were going to achieve A, B, and C; well we achieved A, B, and F, or we achieved none of it, depending upon the outcome of the exercise. Document, identify those gaps, correct the gaps, and then reiterate, go and test again at some point in time, make sure that it's a working document, it's a working plan that is executable when the time comes. Then also, an important distinction to understand is testing vs. exercises. We want to make sure we don't find ourselves in that situation. A test is a pass-fail scenario. An exercise is much harder to measure in that regard, because some elements of an exercise may be successful, some may not, so it's not an entirely pass-fail scenario. It's also good to put out to the organization, when you're conducting these exercises, make sure they understand it's just that, it's not a pass-fail. It takes some of the burden off the employees, and it also makes them not falsely report because no one wants to fail, so, you don't want them just going through and checking boxes just to check the boxes. If something fails, you want to know it fails realistically, so that you can correct. By letting someone know, we're letting the organization know, we're doing an exercise. This is not pass fail, you're not going to get fired, you're not going to have something drastic. It's going to be a learning experience, we expect some things to not work as planned, that's all part of the process, that's why we're testing. It's much better to find out than to think something worked because someone was afraid to say no or afraid to fail, they checked a box even if they didn't do the exercise or do that specific piece, and then find out when the incident happens where the catastrophe is in full swing, that the plan is not executable, so that's not the time to do that.

Chapter 8 Test Scenarios & Simulations

Testing needs to be realistic. Simply reporting back successful testing results is meaningless if the test is not realistic. Something to keep in mind is, we need to make sure that we test the plan. Don't plan the test. What do I mean by that? We need to make it as realistic as possible. In other words, don't let everyone know, hey, the test is coming. The catastrophe's about to arrive on our doorstep Let's go ahead and plan everything to the nth degree. Let's take everything into consideration, let's have all of our resources lined up, let's make sure we have everything in place because in reality, as we know, catastrophes don't announce themselves. They don't knock on the door and say, hey, I'm going to be here tomorrow at 6:00. Everybody get ready. If you want to test the reality and the validity of a test or an exercise, don't plan it to the degree. Throw in some variability. Make sure that you have some things that throw you off to see how the plan functions in a non-perfect world.

Walkthrough Tests
When we're talking about the various types of testing and exercises, we have five that I want to mention here. We have walk-through testing, or walk-through exercises, we have communications,

communication exercises, simulations, we have a partial exercise, and then also a full exercise. Let's take a look at each of these in more detail. For a walk-through, that's a reading through the proposed plan. It's everyone gathering in a room together, or as close together as possible, whether it's over Skype, or some remote communication telepresence, you'll read through the proposed plan, and then you'll ask yourself some questions. Does the plan makes sense? it's a bit of a no brainer, but depending upon who's reading, sometimes people are afraid to speak up, Everyone should be empowered to say, this doesn't make sense, or this isn't valid, or we're missing something here, go through that, that's the purpose of this exercise. Also does it follow a logical path? Are we doing things in the order that we would realistically expect them to either be restored, contained, mitigated. Also, is it understandable and easy to follow for those that must utilize that plan? If it's extremely complicated, full of legalese or ultra-technical jargon, that people reading that plan may or may not be understanding of or may not be privy to that information, it's important to make it understandable. In the middle of a crisis, the brain isn't as loose, it's tightened down, you're in a heightened sense of awareness, stress levels come up, and it becomes a little harder to focus, Making sure these things are easy to understand and easy to follow is critical. Then also revisions may occur numerous times throughout this process because it's not typically a one and done. As we go through this each and every time, it's understood that there's going to be gaps, there's going to be things that are missed, or things that need to be added, so a few revisions of this plan throughout this process or throughout this exercise is expected.

Communication Tests

Next we have communication tests, we want to make sure or ensure that all relevant personnel, all vendors, emergency responders are identified. We need to verify that we have accurate contact information, critical, it does not stay the same typically, and things can change over time, so a periodic review of this information will pay dividends if and when an actual incident occurs. Also identify backups, otherwise known as deputies, for each key position. We don't want to have just one person identified for each specific key role, we need to make sure we have backups for them in case that person is out, unreachable, or they may be affected by the incident, or the catastrophe, or the event, and they can't reply or respond. We need to make sure we have a deputy in that case. Also identify gaps in response times and availability. As we go through this testing, understand are the people in place and is their response realistic? If we expect someone to be able to respond within 30 minutes, and it takes them 6 hours, well, that's not acceptable for this specific scenario. We need to either mitigate that risk, find another person, or adjust the plan to meet those real-world outcomes.

Simulation (Tabletop) Tests

Next, we have simulations. These are also known as tabletop exercises. The objective here is to be as real-world as possible without blowing up the building or having a tornado sweep through. But we want to make sure that we can make it as realistic as possible in a simulated scenario. To do that, we should inject some variability or randomness into the test before. Maybe not have everybody respond. That way, it mirrors what would happen if that specific person or group of people can't respond because the event is impacting them in some way. Also disasters typically don't announce themselves ahead of time. Injecting some type of variability into that test makes it a little bit more real-world and also shows you and the rest of the organization how you can adapt and overcome, still within the parameters of the plan. Because the goal is business continuity. We want to make sure that business can continue, business functions, business services. By doing this, injecting some variability, we ensure an even greater chance of success.

Partial Exercise

Partial exercises are somewhat intrusive so it's going to require people from various areas throughout the organization. Depending upon the size of that company, you may all be located in one location, you may be spread out within a state, throughout the country, or even globally. There may be some disruption as all of these folks are gathered together. You're going to have to coordinate logistically how to make that happen. Some actions will need to be taken that may disrupt normal operations. That's just the nature of the beast. When possible, do these types of exercises when it's least disruptive to the business, after hours, on the weekends. It just depends upon your business and when your busy times are. The goal here is to prepare for disaster recovery up almost to the point of failing over, but not failing over completely, because that would be a full exercise. But we want to take it halfway or three quarters of the way, gaining a much better understanding of how the operation and how the plan functions, but not a full-blown exercise.

Full Exercise

Full exercises are most disruptive to the business. It's a complete testing of the business continuity and disaster recovery plans. It's going soup-to-nuts, from beginning to end, so a complete failover of systems to ensure continuity, again, a continuity of the business, business services. Then, it should be performed, like we talked about with partial exercises, at times that are least intrusive to the company's operations. It could be after hours, over night, weekends, or it may be certain times of the year, maybe there's a slow period. Coordinate that so it's least disruptive, and then you'll ensure the highest chance of participation and buy in, especially from senior management.

Overall Cost and Complexity of Testing
When we're talking about the overall cost and complexity of testing, understand that each one of these different types have a different dollar amount, amount of time, complexity, associated with them. Starting off, we have a walkthrough exercise. Pretty much free, it's just people in a room reading through the exercises, understanding where the gaps are. Not a lot of dollar value, or time. As far as the five different types we're talking about, this is the least cost and the least complex. Next, we have the communications test. We're going to have to test some of our systems, we're going to have to get people engaged from various parts of the business. A little bit more time, a little more complexity; and then we have simulations, partial exercises, and then full exercises. A full exercise is a complete

failover, logistically getting everyone together, staging areas, command center, incident response. It's a lot more to put together, takes a lot more preparation, and it's a lot more complex.

Plan Review and Maintenance
When we're talking about maintaining our business continuity plans, it's very important to review and maintain those plans periodically. Plans should be updated as changes occur, if possible. The size of the organization may dictate that. Well we want to make sure we update these things as often as necessary to make sure the information in the plans are accurate. Business processes, key personnel, vendors and suppliers; all should be updated as things change, because they will change over time. Also, verify contact information. Again, very important, we need to make sure that when we have to go out and call someone, the number doesn't ring back and say, that number's been disconnected, or that's a totally different company because the vendor has changed or has been acquired. It's important that we verify that contact information periodically, update as necessary. Also, site access plans. Have site access plans changed? Have you acquired new buildings? Have you gotten rid of certain facilities. These things need to be up to date as well, and that includes maps, drawings, schematics. All of these things should be included in

our business continuity planning, our business impact analysis, disaster recovery documents; and what that does is it demonstrates a continued due diligence. That's critical to insurers, maybe partners you may be working with, interested parties or stakeholders; all of these things show that you have plans in place to recover from a disaster, continue business. You're much more likely to get insurance, to have third-party folks and vendors work with you. Some insurance companies, some vendors, look for that and require these types of documents to do business with you. It depends upon, again, your industry, but it's a great approach to have this and have it continually updated so that you can show, hey, we take this seriously; it's company wide, we have executive buy-in, and we update our documents periodically, it's not a one and done.

Review Process Outcomes

Next, we want to make sure we do a lessons learned. We want to review that process outcome. That's going to ensure the highest probability of success, our implementation and also our recovery efforts. We need to review and constantly refine over time. That shows continued competency. That's very important for our vendors, insurers, third parties, key stakeholders. Also, it will prepare the organization for either internal or external audits that you may or may not be interested in preparing for certification. Maybe ISO 27001 for cybersecurity or 22301 for business continuity. But, if in fact that is a goal or a requirement for your organization or your industry, having this continued refinement and the reviewing of your processes and your plans will help auditing and also help prepare for those certifications.

Intelligence Lifecycle
When it comes to the intelligence lifecycle, we have the six phases: direction, collection, processing, analysis, dissemination, and feedback. You can look at that as more or less of a loop. It starts off with an evaluation of the environment, understanding what the goals are, the roadmap to get there, and throughout that process, there's a feedback loop. We'll do it at the end, but it can also be done at each stage to make sure the process is functioning as intended, and we're getting the results that we're looking for.

Chapter 9 Threat Intelligence Lifecycle

To put that into a different format, we start off with our objectives and our key questions. That's fed from several things, internal sources, technical sources, and, of course, human sources. Some of it may be automated, some of it may be through manual intervention, talking with other analysts as well, seeing what's happening in their space or in their part of the world. All of these things, again, are fed with threat intelligence. That's comprised of the threat intelligence itself and the various security tools, the SIEM tools, and then also analysts, and that will go back and forth. Those two things feed each other, comprised from these different sources, and making sure we're starting off with understanding what it is we're trying to accomplish, what are our goals and key objectives. All of that then turns around and feeds the actual teams that will go out and utilize that information to defend the network. Incident response teams, it could be security operations, it could be a vulnerability management team, risk analysis team, perhaps maybe a fraud management team, and then, of course, security leadership. We talked about the different teams and why that's important and why they need that information, starting off with defending the actual network, the folks that are on the front lines making sure that these threats are mitigated as much as possible or remediated as quickly as possible, security operations, vulnerability, management, patching, all the way up to security leadership so that they have proper data to make informed decisions of where to invest time, resources, money, infrastructure and so on.

Cyberthreat Intelligence Frameworks
Cyber threat intelligence frameworks, a definition would be: it's a structure for thinking how attackers operate, the methods involved, and where in the overall attack lifecycle that event is occurring. More specifically, that cyber threat intelligence framework allows us to be very prescriptive in how we attack a specific situation. It focuses attention on the proper areas to ensure follow up to make sure eradication and mitigation of future threats. It also provides a common language to communicate internally and also externally, regarding threat details, interrelations between events, and correlations with external data sources. It's a framework that allows us to plug in and understand where something is occurring in the process, focus our resources within that small area rather than trying to take the shotgun approach, allows us to be much more laser-focused on the specific area that needs our attention. That way, we don't waste time, waste effort, and resources working on areas that

don't necessarily matter or perhaps aren't necessarily relevant.

Cyber Kill Chain

The first one I want to call your attention to is something referred to as the Cyber Kill Chain. This was developed by Lockheed Martin in 2011, and it's based upon the military concept of the kill chain. We have seven distinct areas, and it allows us to understand where in the process a specific attack is occurring, whether it's in reconnaissance, weaponization or delivery, but if we understand where in the process that specific attack is, we can focus our resources and our mitigation efforts, and if they have a proper framework, we can understand what actions need to be taken in that area, We can quickly respond. First off, reconnaissance, the adversary is probing for weakness, so such things as harvesting login credentials, or info that can be used for a phishing attack. Next is weaponization, that is creating the deliverable, the payload, using an exploit as a backdoor typically. Delivery is the process of sending that payload to the victim, it could be a malicious email, it could be a thumb drive left, on a desk or on the floor, someone picks it up and says, what's this, next thing mission accomplished, it's been delivered. Then we have exploits, and an exploit is the act of executing the code on the remote system. Installation is the actual installing of malware on that target asset, and it brings us to command and control, or C Squared, or C&C, that creates a channel or persistence where the attacker can control the system remotely. At that point, they have control of perhaps one system, perhaps a number of systems. Then actions, so that's carrying out the intended goal, whether it's encrypting data, destroying data, exfiltrating data. If we can understand where in the process a specific action is, we know how to focus our efforts to quickly shut that thing down. If we can interrupt the chain, the kill chain, if we break that chain just like you break a link in a real life chain, then the chain breaks apart. You can stop it from progressing.

Diamond Model
The diamond model is a complementary model to the cyberthreat kill chain. This was developed by the Center for Cyber Intelligence Analysis and Threat Research. It was designed to track attack groups over time rather than individual attacks. The diamond model states for every intrusion event there exists an adversary that takes a step toward an intended goal by using a capability over infrastructure against a victim to produce a result. What we see is we have this diamond model set up, and you can see we have an adversary, and that can be certain pieces of metadata that we need to

understand about that adversary, their persona, an IP address, network assets, the capabilities that they have, malware, exploits, stolen certificates. We're going to use those capabilities over infrastructure, network assets, devices, domain names to launch some type of an attack on a victim. we need to understand the persona like who that person is, what type of group, what type of industry, role, the persona of that victim, the IP address, network assets. Once we have all these things understood, we can create a persona or an avatar or some type of profile of that person, allow us to understand quickly the types of the remediations that can be put in place to shut those things down. Some of the meta-features that we would also capture to make sure we have data about that specific event in a specific threat group, timestamps, the attack phase, which complements the cyber kill chain, the attack result, the direction, methodology, and resources. Going deep into the diamond model is beyond the scope of this introductory portion, but just understand that these frameworks exist to allow our threat analysis teams to quickly identify where to focus resources and also pass that information on to the defenders that go out and defend against, mitigate or remediate.

MITRE Attack Framework

MITRE is a not-for-profit organization, and they manage federal funding for research projects across multiple agencies. They're responsible for a number of things, some of which you may already be familiar with. For instance, the Common Vulnerabilities and Exposures database, the CVE database. If you've ever done patching, you see the different CVEs that come out and say the CVE and some number attached to it, here's the exposure, here's the vulnerability, here's how you remediate. Also the Common Weaknesses Enumeration or the CWE database. The MITRE ATT&CK framework has a few complementary things that I'd like to call your attention to as well, one of which is the Trusted Automation Exchange of Intelligence Information or TAXII. What this is a transport protocol that allows sharing of threat intelligence information over HTTPS using common APIs and then also Structured Threat Information eXpression or STIX. This is a standardized format for presenting threat intelligence information. It allows different disparate systems to communicate using a common language and exchange information, all with the common goal of eradicating threats as quickly as possible. Just you're aware, the MITRE ATT&CK, the actual name of the framework, stands for adversarial tactics, techniques, and common knowledge. We touched on it again briefly before, but just to dig in a little bit deeper, it is comprised of tactical categories. There's 314 tactics spread across 12 different categories. We have initialize access, execution, persistence, privilege escalation, defense evasion, credential access, discovery, lateral movement, collection, command and control, exfiltration, and then impact. If we understand where something is happening in the cyber kill chain, as an example, and we're able to identify through our threat intelligence analysis what type of threat group is executing or attempting to execute the specific attack, we can use something like the MITRE ATT&CK framework to understand, that specific group uses these x number of tactics, 3, 5, 10, whatever the number might be.

We can quickly focus our attention. We can start enriching that data, pass it on to our defenders so they can go out and do their job of either trying to mitigate or remediate that threat as quickly as possible.

Key Points to Remember

Disaster recovery efforts should be formally started and stopped. People need to know when to start and stop that formal recovery effort. That way they can focus on bringing up secondary systems, recovering full service. If everyone still was under the operating guidelines that it is a recovery effort, they're only going to be focusing on the primary systems. They're not going to be looking at secondary tertiary systems. Once the recovery efforts have stopped, then they can get back to the business of bringing up those other systems as well, and restoring full functionality to the business. Next, tracking systems should also be defined and put in place. Ensure people are accounted for, especially if we have some type of disaster where we have injuries or potentially fatalities. Families notified if applicable, emergency services alerted if required; all of these things should be documented People know how to act, know the steps they're supposed to follow. Then, each tower has a specific area of focus. Executives should address the news media, customers, key stakeholders, as an example. Security will protect corporate assets, our IT admins would bring up key systems, making sure that our data is intact. HR would protect human capital, make sure that those people are accounted for, families notified, hospitals, clinics notified. Then lastly, several call lists should be maintained, and this will go throughout each plan. These things are common to every plan that we develop. That way we can enable quick notification to various groups. We may have an executive call list, then a functional staff, our key people that need to come in away to bring our systems back up and running: managers, supervisors, and maybe a call list for everybody, like a company wide call list. That way we have multiple communication lists that can be triggered or called into action depending upon what needs to be done. We can have different folks focusing on different lists and have them work in tandem. That way, everybody's working in concert to try to get things back up and running as quickly as possible.

Types of Plans
When we're talking about types of plans, there are four categories that we should be aware of. There's incident management, there's business continuity, there's disaster recovery, and then business resumption, business resumption may or could be interchangeable with business continuity, but understand, generally speaking, these are the four categories that your planning will fall into. Plans could be separate and they could be distinct. They don't necessarily have to be one large document, however they certainly could be. It depends upon the size of your company or your organization, how

cohesive the planning is, is it tower by tower or do you have a blanket organizational-wide policy. It just depends upon the individual corporation or the individual company.

Chapter 10 Disaster Recovery & Business Continuity

Disaster recovery plans are similar in scope to business continuity, but it's focused more on information technology. Tasks, action lists, order of recovery. Some of the same things we talked about before, emergency contact information for key personnel, interested parties. Also documentation and references to incident management or command center location because, as we know, information technology, or IT, doesn't necessarily, and quite often does not, sit where corporate sits. It may be in a remote data center, it may be some other location. The things that may be readily apparent to the business, like incident management or command center location, may not necessarily be readily apparent to IT folks. It has to be documented, and we have a standardized way of going through these things. Also, activities associated with people, process, and technology. But again, remember, this is for IT-related activities, not necessarily the initial incident management or initial business recovery efforts

Business Continuity Plan
Business continuity plans deal with the resumption and recovery of business operations once the initial

disruption is contained. The incident management plan will deal with the immediate. And then once the bleeding is stemmed, we can move on to business continuity efforts, recovery efforts. How to begin recovery is a key element of the plan, again all of these things will be documented, location of key personnel and key resources, disaster recovery locations or alternate work locations, staging areas. Also, needed resources, whether it be supplies, logistics, interested parties, stakeholders. Also, standardized data collection and reporting templates, forms, portals. How will people start to do their work, do they need to go to a specific location or a portal or fill out a form if they need supplies, how do they request assistance?

Business Resumption Plan
Business resumption plans can be the same or part of the business continuity plan. It doesn't have to be, it can be a separate document, but keep in mind these things could be one and the same. It defines who owns the resumption process because, keep in mind, it may be different than the people who are responsible for incident management or disaster recovery. It may be a separate team. We may have business folks coming in and spinning and owning the business resumption process, processes for determining the replacement of staff, if necessary, perhaps even buildings, depending on how bad the

incident was, infrastructure, things could be damaged, compute network storage, power, heating, cooling, HBAC, our heating, ventilation, air conditioning units, also services. It just depends upon the nature of the incident and the scope of damage.

Incident Management Plan

When it comes to an incident management plan, it's going to deal with the initial response to an incident, so that means tasks, and the actions, and the priorities that which things should be addressed. What do I need to do specifically immediately after an incident happens? How do I triage that event? Emergency contact details of key personnel and interested parties, or stakeholders, activities required as it relates to people, process, and technology. This is limited in scope to the things we need to do immediately, not necessarily long term. This is incident management. We need to contain the existing incident, and then we can move on to recovery efforts. Also contact guidelines, internal contacts, media, emergency responders, that's going to include documentation, maps, charts, maybe third-party response details, site access info, especially if we have geo-dispersed locations, and we need to understand how to get into specific locations, what's the best way to get in, get out. Then insurance contact and claim procedures, which is always high on everyone's list of favorite things to do, but dealing with insurance companies, especially if it's a major incident, is particularly helpful if you start documenting from the beginning, so you don't leave anything out or it doesn't get misconstrued.

Data Retention
When it comes to data retention, there's a number of reasons why data may need to be retained, or not be retained, there's various reasons for either side of this coin. It could be for compliance, it could be for eDiscovery, for data mining, to understand customer history, or to improve the customer experience. However, there also may be implications for keeping data too long. Some companies don't want to store data after a certain period of time, just to get rid of data that's no longer necessary, to prune their data to save on storage costs. The longer the data's retained, those costs and storage requirements, they increase, because things start to accumulate over time. Proper data governance helps with this, and when we're talking about data retention, there are a number of options, there's a number of ways to skin the cat, so to speak. Replicating offsite is one option, whether that be a remote data center or a cloud provider, so that can protect against disaster, a smoking hole incident where the entire data

center goes out, cyber incidents, ransomware attacks, breaches. If we're replicating to another location, that can help guard against those types of incidents. As an example, we have a user, and she is accessing using some data, using an application. Well that data is stored in her primary location, her primary data center. There may be primary storage that that network or that system is attached to, and that's fine. She's pulling data off of that primary storage, but, we need to make sure that that's protected. Typically, that storage will be offloaded to a backup device, or backup arrays, so that is off of primary storage, it's on backups, but, it's still sitting in the primary data center. That solves for the problem of if the array were to go out, but it doesn't solve against the problem of what if the data center goes away, we have some type of disaster. We have a couple options. From there, we could backup to a cloud provider. That could be AWS, it could be Google, and it could be Azure. There are a number of options. There are a lot of other providers as well, those are the big three, and then there's hot storage, things that have a higher degree of performance, it's not going to be as good as onsite performance, but it's still there. Or if it's long-term storage, you could even push it down to a lower level of storage within that cloud provider. As an example, AWS has a service called Glacier, which is a very cheap and deep storage, but it's not very responsive, but, it's there for long-term retention. Alternatively, we could replicate to a remote data center. It's something that we own, and in doing so, we maintain that geographic dispersal. If something were to go wrong, a power outage or some type of disaster at our primary data center, we have that data replicated offsite somewhere. A third option might be to have those backups stored on tape, and have those tapes physically transported to a storage facility. The more modern ways, however, will be to replicate either to a cloud or a remote data center.

Putting It All Together
Proper procedures, documentation, and of course, practice, - all of these things together heightens the degree of success when responding to incidents. Because unfortunately, it's not a matter of if something happens, it's more likely a matter of when. It just becomes more and more frequently, unfortunately, more or less as the cost of doing business almost. There are a number of teams that would be involved when dealing with an incident. We have executive management. We have business leadership and the various lines of business. There will be leadership from various areas, not just one group. Typically, it's going to be a number of groups from different types of businesses or lines of business, depending upon the nature of the breach, what applications and services it affects. Then we

have IT operations and infrastructure, they're the folks that will be responsible for getting all these things back up and running, and then we have security operations, who will be heavily involved in analyzing and making sure that these things are covered going forward. We have engineering, which may need to change the way that things are done, depending upon, The nature of the breach, the application, maybe there's a hole or something that needs to be patched; and then DevOps, potentially, depending upon the nature of the breach. Do you have to change something in your CI/CD pipeline? All of those types of things. Each of these groups, as you may imagine, have sub components. If we dig into security operations as an example, here we have our CISO sitting at the head of the organizational chart, but there's a number of groups under them: risk management, identity management, security operators, security architecture; and each of those have separate subgroups. Your organization may not necessarily be this large or it may be bigger, it just depends, but there are detection, prevention, incident handling, and even within incident handling, we have forensics and incident management, and incident response teams. Again, if it's a large organization, you may have all of these or more, if it's a very small group, you may have one person wearing all of these hats, it just depends. Digging in just a bit further, we can see we have, under detection we might have security event triage, and security analysts, and then hunt operations and intelligence, threat intelligence analysis, and then we might have security administrators and security engineering. I'm just trying to give you an idea that there's a number of people that may be involved when handling a breach. No need to necessarily understand each of these down to the nth degree, just understand that it's not necessarily just a one person operation unless you're a very, very small company. There's a lot of coordination that takes place when an incident occurs.

Example Process
Let's say unfortunately the inevitable has happened, and a Coffee shop has a breach. So once that happens, a number of things need to take place. Initially we'll have the alert, and that could be from an automated alert from one of our seen systems or some type of monitoring system. We have IOCs, or indicators of compromise, that are observed. It could be an outage that's reported, it could be customer-reported degradation of apps or services, so on. There's some reason why we're alerted to that breach. From there, we're going to have to jump into action and analyze what's taking place. That consists of a number of things, again identifying the issue, understanding what is taking

place, take corrective actions as quickly as possible, that's feasible, without going overboard. We need to engage proper teams very quickly to make sure they're aware, they're spinning themselves up, and we begin communications. From there, the communications take place, and that goes amongst a number of groups. It goes through management, it goes through business partners, peer groups, potentially customers, the media, it could even be law enforcement, and of course vendors. Depending upon the nature of the breach, we may need to bring vendors in very quickly to help us recover or to harden the systems, potentially even bring in additional equipment depending on how big and how widespread that breach is. All of these things are happening in parallel, so this is not necessarily a serial timeline, it's not one after the other, a number of these things will start to spin up in parallel, and you'll have to have someone that sits at the head of that in your command center and coordinates all of these efforts? We've talked about all of these things before, but just understand that there are a number of things that take place at the same time when we're dealing with these types of breaches. So from there, we have to recover and then harden those systems, so that may be rebuilding those systems, restoring from backup, in some form or fashion, we need to recover those systems, validate that those systems are in fact functional, and again that's going to be spinning up a bridge, having all the different app teams involved, having those guys and girls all on the phone saying yes, we're back up online, or yes, I can perform action A, B, and C, so the application is recovered. And then from there, we would take preventative corrections, and then monitor to make sure that things are working, that the corrections work. We want to make sure we don't just bring the system back and leave it in exact same state it was before. We need to make sure that we take preventive action, harden that system, if possible, to make sure if that same type of attack were to occur again, we're protected against that attack. And then we need to make sure that we document and do an AIR, or after incident review, or a peer incident review, or whatever it may be called in your specific organization, but you should do that after the fact, you can review what you've done, lessons learned? Lessons learned, the steps that were taken, also communicate with executives, so they have a level of comfort around the incident, understanding that we have a handle on things, and then and after-incident review, so that we can understand across all the different teams that are involved, what happened, how we can respond better, or perhaps quicker the next time. And then in reality, we want to make sure that we audit the environment. Audit for similar gaps in other systems, and ensure that those corrective actions or corrective measures that we took on that one system or that one application are applied consistently throughout the environment? We want to make sure that we're patching all of our systems that are similar, maybe the same operating system, or the same code level, depending upon what the actual gap was, where the vulnerability was, we need to make sure that we're patching against that across the environment. And then lastly, develop new MOPs, or methods of procedures, so that way we have a documented way of moving forward, ensuring that those best practices are applied when new systems are built and brought into the environment. In this chapter, we talked about a number of things including incident response plans and process, we talked about various testing exercises, walk throughs, tabletops, simulations. We talked about the various attack frameworks, the MITRE framework, Diamond Model. We talked about stakeholder management and also communication plans, disaster recovery, and business continuity plans, along with continuity of operation planning, and then various incident response teams, retention policies, data of retention, and then responding to an incident, putting it all together and understanding all of the various teams that need to be spun up, how things happen in parallel, not necessarily a serial process, and how we get things back up online, communicate properly to all the teams involved, and restore our systems, patching and documenting, making sure that doesn't happen again in the future.

Chapter 11 How to Implement Data Sources to Support an Investigation

In this chapter, we'll be covering Understanding Appropriate Data Sources to Support an Incident. We'll be talking about vulnerability scans and the output, what we do with those outputs. We'll talk about SIEM and SIEM dashboards. We'll talk about log files and how they can support an investigation or data analysis, trying to figure out what happened, where, when, why and how. We'll talk about syslog, rsyslog, and syslog-ng or next generation. We'll talk about the differences there. We'll also talk about something called journal control or journalctl, nxlog. We'll talk about retention for basic things like email, audit logs. Then we'll talk about bandwidth monitors, metadata, and how it changes for different types of files. We'll talk about NetFlow and sFlow, the differences between the two, and then a little bit about protocol analyzers and outputs. When we're talking about accessing all of these different types of data, interpreting assessment results, understanding what's going on, the amount of data that's being created is increasing exponentially, so the amount of sensors, telemetry data. Security tools, analyzers, packet sniffers, all of these things, they generate a massive amount of data. Part of the job is to filter through all of that data and to find out what's relevant, to filter through the noise. Relevance is different for each environment, so it's not going to be a one size fits all. Something that may be normal in one environment could be abnormal in another and vice versa. It's important to understand what is normal for your specific environment. Also, understand what is the goal of the tool or what is the goal of the assessment? What are we looking to gather when we're sifting through all of this data. Then automate where possible. Automation is going to be key here because we want to be able to trigger an alert when a real issue occurs and then filter through all the noise. Filtering through the noise boils down to establishing a security baseline. That's going to help us understand what's normal. This will apply to no matter what the environment is, whether we're doing packet sniffers or a SIEM dashboard or any type of telemetry data. Once we understand what is normal, then we can very quickly or at least more quickly understand what's abnormal. This enables an analyst to quickly see anomalies and deviations from normal. If you understand what's normal, if you see a spike that's not normal, we see a spike in the middle of the night or a spike on a specific port or a spike on a specific type of application that's not normally doing that, then that can alert us to some type of abnormal activity, potentially an indicator of compromise. There are tools that can automate data collection and simplify that task, and we'll talk about a few of those in just a moment. But, we want to alert when a threshold is reached X amount of times within a certain interval. Rather than every single time a threshold is breached, that's going to create a ton of noise because things can spike constantly. If it's an intermittent spike or a one-off, we don't necessarily want to be notified of that. If we have something down the road that becomes a problem, we can go back historically and look for the one-offs and maybe see a trend over time. But every single time something hits a threshold, we don't want to necessarily be alerted by that. By creating these baselines and then setting thresholds or triggers, if X amount of triggers within a certain time interval, that will help us to filter through the noise. One of those tools that can help us is something referred to as a vulnerability scanner, and a vulnerability scanner can determine where there are gaps in defenses. There are a lot of them out there. They all have similar functionality, but some of the more well-known ones are OpenVAS or GVM, Nessus, Retina, Nmap, SAINT. There are a number of other ones as well. I'm not necessarily recommending or endorsing one over the other. Just understand that generally speaking, vulnerability scanners give us a lot of information about our environment. They allow us to scan the environment for vulnerabilities, for gaps in our defenses, if you will. As an example, GVM is a vulnerability scanner that does a number of different things. It gives us a number of vulnerabilities, but it allows us to scan our environment, scan all the different devices within our environment, and then show what gaps exist, if any, on those different pieces of equipment, those different nodes in our environment, whether it's a Linux server, Windows server, some type of endpoint. So from there, once the vulnerability is discovered, we can drill down, see all about that vulnerability, see what the potential severity is, and then potential remediations. It allows us to stack rank what's in the environment and then remediate appropriately.

SIEM

SIEM is the security information and event management system. What this does is do a bit of data aggregation and correlation, doing automated alerting and triggers, time synchronization, event deduplication, and then logs that are in a WORM format or write once, read many. A SIEM platform, is a security tool that allows us to aggregate data from a number of different sources, and it correlates that data to make it easy to identify when things happen. We can look at things from a number of different parameters, whether it be CPU utilization, network utilization. Let's take a look at this in a little more detail. Here we have one called Metricbeat from Elastic, and it's being displayed in Kibana.

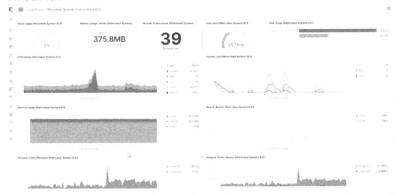

This is a dashboard, and it shows us a number of different things. Memory usage, number of processes, disk usage metrics, and this is for a specific host. But then it also show us the I/O on that specific host, the network traffic, and this can be used to look at individual hosts on a network. It can be used to look at switches and routers, to look at network flow. It gives us a lot of insight into the network, and then we can drill down, and you can see we're looking at the same time slices across all of these different metrics. It allows us to correlate that data and make sure we're understanding what's happening from a global perspective. And if we drill down a bit, we see that we have CPU usage, also system load.

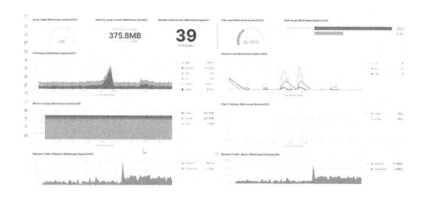

We can see a spike here around 15:15 or 3:15 in the afternoon, and we can see there's a spike. If we click on that, highlight that area and drill down, we can look in the logs for that specific event and see in more detail what's happening. We can search for specific parameters, we can look at anomalies in the network, or we can browse through to see if anything stands out. If we look at this in more detail, we have a graphical representation of a SIEM correlation dashboard. We have application, network, storage, firewall, and compute, and we have a time scale. We can see that is traffic. There's activity on various metrics within this correlated dashboard. Well let's say, for instance, we see this, and then all of a sudden the next day or, let's say, the time slices that we see here represented are the next 12 hours as an example. But we see this generic data. Nothing necessarily stands out. For this example, this could be considered a baseline, and nothing stands out. However, if we then see a spike pop up, and we see a lot of increased traffic, a lot of increased activity, disk I/O, firewall utilization, we can then drill down on each of those specific metrics and see what, in fact, is happening. These could be indicators of compromise. We could see that they could potentially be doing some type of data exfiltration or some type of Smurf attack or amplification attack, some type of breach into the network or least trying to do some type of denial-of-service or distributed denial-of-service attack. These types of things, this correlation engine, allows us to correlate across a number of different metrics and see the trending and then see the aggregate total because if we're looking at just one of these metrics, it may or may not stand out as an anomaly. But if we're looking at it across the board, and we can see well normally it looks like this. But today, for some reason or a couple hours later, it should look like this, but it's jumped up. Those things stand out immediately as red flags. It allows us to go and drill in deeper to see what's going on.

Log Files
Next we have log files, and log files can be a rich source of information. Or they could be ridiculously boring and put you to sleep. It just depends upon how you use the log files, what types of tools you have to parse through them, what automation you

may have in place. But, it is a very rich source of information and can be used for many purposes, including audits for discovering IOCs or indicators of compromise. It can be used for forensic investigations, general alerting. There's a number of different types of log files, all of which have various nuances, but we have log files for network traffic, for system utilization, application logs, security logs, web, DNS, authentication logs, log ons, log offs, dump files. We could have VoIP and call manager logs, session initiation protocol or SIP traffic logs. All of these things can prove very valuable when we need to investigate some type of breach or some type of incident. I will say that when you do log, you have to be very careful not to log too much because if you generate just too much noise, then it becomes pretty much just that, noise. By the same token, if you log too little or if you audit too little, then you have a false sense of security thinking that you're capturing the information that you need. But then when something happens, you either don't have that information readily available, or you don't have it in which case, then you start to get calls from VPs and executive management and say, I need that information and you're like oops, well, I don't have it. That, as you could imagine, is a lonely place to be and not somewhere that we want to be. We want to make sure that we proactively adjust and identify what we need to log, that we store it property, that we audit and retain that information long enough so that it retains its value, but not indefinitely so that it becomes, again, just noise or things that we're never going to look at and it just takes up space, which, everything reverts back to things cost money. Storage costs money. Getting back to the previous example, we may see a spike in traffic. We might see a spike of activity, and it's correlated across our network. Not necessarily just on a specific host. It could also be on the network, the firewall. Well, using our logs and analysis tools, we can dig in, pull in event IDs, log files that are stored on the server, in this case a DNS server, and we can see there are a number of hits for two different ports.

That is an anomaly that's not necessarily normal for that environment. That would be potentially an indicator of compromise and would require further investigation. In this case, it's quite possible that someone's trying to do some type of data exfiltration through our DNS channels or some other type of malicious activity. All of these tools allow us to continually drill in. If we double-click down even further, we can see that in this specific instance, the DNS server encountered a domain name packet exceeding the maximum length in the packet. And it shows the event ID, it shows the IP address. All of these things can be used to identify indicators of compromise. It's not normal, it's not something that we see every day, and it's an anomaly. In this case, someone is trying to breach the network, and it would require again further examination. In the real world when something like this happens, depending upon the size of your organization, you may or may not be doing this yourself. You may be a junior analyst, and you would pass this on further up the chain for further investigation. You might have a network security team. You might have the server admins themselves, the DNS administrators. They may jump in and start trying to identify where that traffic is coming from. You'll have server admins, you might have virtualization admins, the network folks, firewall folks, and, of course, security personnel. You might spin up a war room and have everyone sit around the table and everyone looking at the same thing at the same time. They may all be together trying to understand what in fact is happening. Log files become critical in that case. Everyone can look at the data historically, and you can look back a day, a week, a month, depending upon how long you retain that data, and understand what is normal and what's not normal. Is this something that happens once a week? Is this something that happens once a month? Or is this the first time it's ever happened? By getting a bit of a historical view of events, it helps to identify how serious something may or may not be. It could be just someone probing, just seeing if they can get what they can get, and just doing some general reconnaissance. Or, it could be a targeted attack, which would warrant much more of a response.

Log Management, Syslog, Rsyslog, and Syslog-ng
When it comes to log management, log management can help reduce complexity, it can help reduce cost', and increase speed on ingestion for downstream consumers. What do I mean by that? Well, data quality, normalizing, parsing, and filtering out the noise, the uninteresting traffic, that's a big time saver. It gives us information that is usable, actionable. It also helps with cost reduction. We can optimize our SIEM, we can reduce storage, and also ingestion costs because depending upon the platform that we choose, it can be costly to just

bring in data from various sources. If we can parse that further upstream, get rid of the things that aren't necessarily interesting, then we're only paying for what we're consuming or ingesting. And then also security, we can encrypt data both in motion and also at rest. As an example, here we have a number of things that are producing log files, firewalls, applications, it can be compute network logs, storage logs. All of those things can then be put into a syslog server, a relay or a server, in this case syslog-ng, and then forward it on to whatever applications we want to use or have be the consumer of those specific log feeds, and it could be Splunk, it could be ELK, Kafka, it could be Hadoop, databases, so on, and so on. There are a number of things we can feed those different log files to. syslog-ng, as an example, allows us to do that. If we wanted to install syslog-ng into our system, as an example, here we have a Kali Linux session open, and from a terminal, I can just do a sudo apt-get install, and then choose syslog-ng, and a from there it's going to ask me do I want to do this, and of course the answer is yes. Then it's going to pull down the files, takes a few moments, it'll read through the database, then it'll install the various sub files, and within a matter of, say, a minute or so, we're done.

When it comes to syslog,syslog-ng, and also
something called rsyslog, a few things that I just
want to make sure that you're aware of. Syslog was
developed in 1980, so it's been quite a while, but
it's a tried and true mechanism. It was developed
initially as part of the send mail implementation for
collecting system logs. It was UDP only, User
Datagram Protocol, which is a connectionless
delivery system, so there's no guaranteed delivery,
and it operated on port 514. Years later in 1998,
syslog-ng comes out. That extended the
functionality of syslog by adding TCP, or
Transmission Control Protocol, which is a
connection-oriented delivery mechanism,
content-based filtering, database logging features,
and also TLS encryption. Then roughly about 6 years
later, as a competitor to syslog-ng, rsyslog came
out, and that extended syslog functionality even
further by adding buffered operation support. If
connectivity was lost, it could still buffer on the
client until connectivity was re-established. That
buffered operation support and then also RELP, or
RELP, protocol, which is Reliable Event Logging
Protocol, so that made for a much more robust
delivery system. It was guaranteed, or at least we
knew when messages weren't delivered, so it could

retry again. These types of things are used by like the financial industry, things that cannot tolerate dropped messages. Just understand that there are a few different variations of syslogging, whether it's syslog, syslog-ng, or rsyslog, all have the same basic features; however, with each iteration, new features are added.

Journalctl

Next, let's talk about a tool called journalctl, and what journalctl is is a Linux command to view systemd, kernel, and also journal logs, and allows us to parse through those things, configure the output. We can search through all entries, we can look for entries by keyword, by type, by date, and then also output to a file, or also to a JSON format. It gives us a lot of options when parsing through system logs. To use the command, we can open up a terminal, and type sudo journalctl, and we'll want to use sudo in this case, so that we get all the messages, including kernel messages. And if we didn't do sudo, we wouldn't get all of the messages displayed to us.

So from there, sudo journalctl, and from there, we can parse through all of the entries in the log, and there a number of options that we can use to show just kernel messages, just messages since last boot, by a certain date or time, so on and so on. Let's take a look at this in action and get a little more detail here. So from a terminal, again, I will run journalctl, and that gives me all of the current information. If you do sudo journalctl, and then as new entries are added, that log file gets updated in real time. I'll open up another window, and just do a quick check on my GVM setup that we installed previously. As that happens, you'll notice, as I'm running commands, and I'll pull it off-screen for just a moment, but as I run commands, you'll see the log files get updated. Since I'm following the journal, anytime anything happens, any entries get put in, it gets updated in real time. I can also turn around and say journalctl -n, and give it a number for 10, Just 10 entries, and then put in the output and make it json-pretty. It formats that output, rather than the line-by-line that we just saw, and it formats it, quote/unquote pretty, giving it the proper coding, the proper indentation. just scratching the surface of what journalctl can do, but it gives us a lot of flexibility in parsing our logs, searching for specific events, formatting the output.

```
^C
kali@kali:~$ sudo journalctl -n 10 -o json-pretty
```

And, as usual within Linux, if there's something that you're not sure of, or you need to know a command, we can always do what pretty much every guy doesn't want to do, and that is read the

118

manual. But, journalctl, journal c-t-l, --help, will give us all the commands that are available.

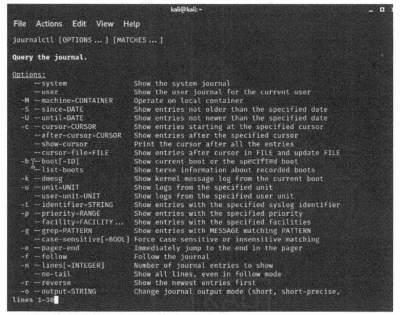

You can see, we can do things like -b. That will give us the current boot or specified boots. We could put a --boot -1 to show us just the kernel messages from the last boot. We can look at things like priority range, or we can grep for a specific pattern. That way we can show messages that only match a specific thing that we may be looking for. We also, -f, or follow, and that will follow the journal. It will show the most recent entries, and then anything new that gets added as we go. we just scroll down, we can keep seeing there are many, many options here available to us. We can do merge, we can output to a file, we can show the disk usage, the total disk usage for all of the journal files. We can vacuum the journal, reduce the size and delete older entries. We can flush the journal from any point in time, and so on. I encourage you to go against your intuition and read the manual on these things, because a lot of times, there's some useful information in here that you wouldn't necessarily know unless you dig in under the covers just a bit. Poke through this when you have an opportunity, and familiarize yourself with the options available.

NXLOG

One other log and aggregation platform that I want you to be familiar with is something called NXLog. This is a multi-OS log aggregation and collection platform. It can collect and aggregate from Windows, from Linux, Mac, even Solaris. And we can also aggregate, filter, and enrich that data and then integrate with other SIEM software. I'm not going to dig into too, too much there, but just be aware that it is a multi-platform collection and aggregation tool and also integrates with SIEM software. It pulls all those different files together, all those log files from different operating systems, collects it, aggregate that data, and then passes it on to SIEM software or some other platform for further usage and consumption.

Chapter 12 Retention Auditing, Compliance & Metadata

We have all of this auditing information, What do we do with it? Retention policies should be defined and may be mandated by certain compliance regulations. When it comes to auditing, we need to determine what is most valuable when auditing that information. If we audit too much, if we collect too much, then it becomes noise, and it becomes limited in value because we just have so much stuff, it's too hard to sift through. That's where taking some time to clearly define what we want to audit and why and then how long are we going to retain that data for. That way we balance between the amount of data that we collect and the amount of time that we're collecting it for. It probably doesn't do us much good to go back 8 years, 10 years for something for a log on or log off. But yet, 2 or 3 days is probably too short. Maybe 2 weeks, a month, a month and a half? It just depends upon your environment. It depends upon what you're auditing for. But you definitely want to make sure that you clearly define it, and it's going to be a group effort here. You might have security folks, you might have administrators collectively understanding what it is we're logging for and how long we're going to keep it. Then we talk about compliance. There are certain things, certain regulatory bodies or local laws that may require data be retained for a certain period of time. That will vary by location. There is no or wrong answer across the board. Make sure you check with your local municipality, local, state, federal, or whatever country may be residing in, make sure that those things are in compliance and that you're retaining that information for the required period of time if applicable. Then for investigations, good data is critical to investigations on incidents, breaches. It could be criminal activity, it just could be malicious activity, or it just could be an anomaly that you need to investigate. Logs, audit data, file metadata, all of these things are very critical when we're trying to determine what happened, who did what, where, when, why, and how. Preservation of evidence is critical. Chain of custody is critical. Not Much just for an internal investigation, but chain of custody becomes crucial if those things ever need to go to court for prosecution.

Bandwidth Monitors

What a bandwidth monitor does, as the name implies, it's going to monitor network traffic and overall bandwidth. It can identify anomalies if we have some type of spike on the network or something that's not normal. We can identify IOCs or indicators of compromise potentially. It doesn't necessarily mean that all IOCs will come through this type of monitoring tool, but it certainly can be a help in that regard. Such things as data exfiltration, we can see things that aren't necessarily normal and identify those trends and those one-offs or the spikes. Then unusual traffic in general, the type, the source, the destination, or perhaps the application. All of these different things can appear once we understand what's normal. If we have a baseline and we establish what is normal, then it's very easy or at least I should say easier for us to identify what is not normal. We can see just a normal amount of traffic, whether it be network, storage, compute. All of a sudden, we see a spike, and then we can go hey, wait a minute. What's going on here? And it gives us an opportunity to then drill down and look in deeper to see what's going on. That's where log files come into play. That's where our aggregation and collection things come into play, our SIEM software. All of these things work in tandem to help us identify IOCs. We'll talk about NetFlow and sFlow here in just a moment, which can also function as bandwidth monitors and help us understand the flows between the different nodes and endpoints on our network.

Metadata
Metadata is data about data. It's data that provides information about other data. That means different

things in different context. For email, as an example, an email header can show things like the sender info, the date and time, the IP addresses that it came from or the hops that it went through as it gets from point A to point B, the intermediary hosts. All of this metadata can become important when we're trying to understand where things are coming from. If we're getting a lot of spam, perhaps malicious activity, malware, that metadata around that email can become very, very valuable for investigations. How about for mobile devices? Details about phone calls or messages, perhaps location or GPS information, all of these things can divulge information about a caller, even medical information, associations. When it comes to the web, we can use metadata to optimize for web sites, but it can also be used in a not-so-nice way. It can be used to identify visitors. We can fingerprint their browsers, look at certain things within the screen resolution and the fonts that are installed. All of the different graphical back-end pieces that don't necessarily or aren't necessarily visible to the end user can be used to fingerprint that browser and identify that person. If they visit again using that browser, even if it's from a different IP address, you could identify that person based upon those web browser metadata characteristics. Metadata can be good in a lot of instances. It can be not so good like for advertisers, and spammers. Then it can also be used maliciously to identify things or give away information that we don't necessarily want to become public knowledge or have visible to other users. Then we're talking about file metadata. So file attributes can identify, the owner of that file or the author, the date and time it was created or modified, the word count, even GPS coordinates if it's a photograph and, the type of device used, the type of camera, the f-stop, the aperture, all of these things can be pulled from the metadata on specific types of files. But this EXIF information, the GPS coordinates, it's important to understand that as you upload pictures to social media or send from one person to another, if you don't remove that information, it's quite possible that that actual metadata information gets passed along with that file as well. So keep those things in mind and understand that if you don't want this information to become public knowledge or at least associated with that specific file, then remove those properties whenever possible.

Netflow, sFlow, and IPFIX

NetFlow is a way of monitoring our network, and it takes it a step further, than just looking at typical network monitoring, as it will group the communication between two hosts on a network into flows? It's not just simple packet capturing. It's grouping that into flows to give you a more holistic view of traffic on your network. We have a few things in place here. We have a router, which is typically where you're going to have NetFlow enabled. That's going to be a NetFlow exporter, and that's going to be connecting to various networks, whether it be the internet, remote sites, a LAN, a WAN. Then we're going to be connecting to a NetFlow connector, and we'll have an administrator console where you can see a graphical representation, an application that will take the NetFlow data that's exported from the NetFlow exporter and display it graphically. We also have flow storage that's connected to the NetFlow connector. So, we have NetFlow packets of flow from the router to the collector, and then we also have the administrator that will query the collector. One's feeding data into the collector, one's accessing or querying data from the collector. The collector and the storage itself are collectively known as the NetFlow cache. As we enable NetFlow on the various devices in our network, one thing just to keep in mind is that each device should have its own separate port number. We can have multiple devices in the network reporting into or sending data to a NetFlow collector. Just make sure that each one has its own port number so that the NetFlow collector can differentiate between. Otherwise, the collector won't know what's what, and it would just group everything together and give you bad data or a bad view of what's happening on the network. Some data that is collected by a NetFlow collector would be the source and destination IP address, the IP protocol field value, source and destination port numbers, also counters, whether it be packets or bytes, timestamps, the start time and end time, and then also where observed, the interface and the direction, whether it's ingress or egress and whether it's unidirectional or bidirectional. And just for your own knowledge, there's two main flavors of NetFlow. We have version 5 and version 9, with version 9 being the newer one. And the other implementations that we'll talk about, sFlow and IPFIX, are based off of NetFlow version 9 as well. There's a similar implementation called sFlow, and we'll talk about some of the differences here. With NetFlow, its Cisco proprietary, meaning it only works or functions on Cisco gear, and more granular collection of IP traffic to create flows. It does it packet by packet. We can get very granular. It only collects IP traffic, however, and we'll notice the differentiation here in just a moment. It's a more detailed collection, but it's also more CPU and resource intensive. Then, if we want to display that data graphically, we'll need a third-party collector such as SolarWinds, PRTG. And it's comprised of two components, the exporter and then the cache or the analyzer. As far as sFlow is concerned, that was introduced by HP in 1991, years after NetFlow came out. It samples packets and counters to create flows similarly to what NetFlow does. But the distinction here being that it's samples, so it doesn't do it packet by packet by packet. By sampling, we're getting more of a trend, but it's also less resource intensive. It potentially scales better. It also can collect traffic from OSI layers 2 through 7. It's not just IP traffic. It doesn't provide as detailed packet-level information as NetFlow, but it samples the data, and that's configurable, how often it samples, so that it has the ability to scale. All devices need to be sFlow compatible, so that's something to keep in mind. Then also, two components, an agent and a collector. There are some similarities between the two. Then we've evolved into a new standard called IPFIX, and that stands for Internet Protocol Flow Information Export. That is a collector export protocol, and it's based on NetFlow version 9. All of the features that you would see in NetFlow, however, it's not Cisco proprietary. It's nonproprietary. It also does packet count, byte count, type of service, flow direction, and routing domain. A lot of good information there. That allows you to monitor your network, see what types of services are running, what are the top sites, the top domains, who's the top talkers? It allows you to go in and get very granular with the network and understand what's going on. If you have lags or if you have applications that are performing poorly, these are, of course, good reasons to use NetFlow or IPFIX. It can be used for network monitoring, for measurement. It can be used for threat detection, and then also, some service providers will use it for accounting and billing purposes as well. All three are great tools. They need to be implemented on the devices in the network, and then all the devices that you're monitoring need to be compatible. You configure the exporters of the agents to report to a collector, and then you can go with an analyzer or a dashboard, and then get all the information that we talked about before about how your network is functioning.

Detecting an Amplification Attack (ICMP echo)
We've talked about Smurf attacks, and we've talked about amplification attacks. What I wanted to talk about real briefly here is how we could use NetFlow or sFlow to help thwart a Smurf attack, or an amplification attack. If you recall, with a Smurf attack, otherwise known as an amplification attack, a hacker would send a directed broadcast with the victim's IP spoofed to a network segment, to the broadcast IP address on a network segment so that everybody on that network would get that request, but instead of replying back to the attacker they would reply back to the victim and flood that

person's machine or that server or whatever the intended victim is. So here we have all of the different computers attached to the network. Once that spoofed ICMP echo is sent they all reply back to the victim's computer again, a victim's PC, desktop, laptop, or a server, depending upon what the target is, that can potentially overrun the host system, the amplification attack, if you have enough hosts on that network. Because, again, it could be dozens, it could be hundreds, or it could be thousands of computers all replying back to that specific victim. Using NetFlow or sFlow, or another network monitoring solution for that matter, but since we're talking about NetFlow and sFlow it makes sense to cover that here. What we could do is use NetFlow or, again, sFlow to identify ICMP echo requests or these pings, these Smurf attacks or these amplification attacks to detect that network attack. We could identify the victim using traffic monitoring to identify top destinations for ICMP echo responses. We could identify that within the tool. From there we could use NetFlow or sFlow to filter for the top subnets sourcing ICMP echo responses. We could then identify the port used for ICMP echo response to enter the site or to enter our network by using, again, NetFlow or sFlow to show top router and switch ports, receiving ICMP echo requests and packets destined for that specific victim, and then we can create an ACL filter on the router or the switch port to block ICMP traffic from the source subnet. Just a quick example of how we might use this tool. Automate to some degree, create filters and triggers so if these things happen we can be alerted, and either automate that process and automate that response or at least become aware of it, and then manually investigate and intervene as necessary.

Protocol Analyzer Output
Let's now talk about protocol analyzers and a little bit about what they do. A protocol analyzer is a packet inspection tool, and there are ones out there like Wireshark, which is probably one of most popular ones. It's an open source packet analyzation or packet analyzer tool. Retina, Nessus, Nmap can also be used to map protocols and see what protocols are available, what ports are open. And it can be used to troubleshoot network issues. It could be used to detect or inspect indicators of compromise and even decrypt SSL transmission if you import the certificates into Wireshark and use those to decrypt the traffic that you're capturing. Just to give you an idea though of what it can and can't do, here are some common use cases, and the one that I will draw your attention to is where it says spy on other network users. You can collect sensitive information, such as login details, users cookies depending upon the content and the

encryption methods that they may use. A lot of it is done for legitimate purposes. But protocol analyzers can also be used to sniff traffic and gather information on other users. It can be used for good and used for bad. Not intending to make you a Wireshark professional at this point, but I just want to introduce you to the tool. Understand that protocol analyzers can give you a lot of deep, deep information about communication on your network. You can go in and examine packets. You can look at the actual flow of information. You can follow it back and forth. And it gives you a great amount of detail from a security professional's perspective, but also for network analyzation. Network professionals look at it for troubleshooting applications, for troubleshooting network performance, seeing where things might get held up. Maybe packets are dropped quite a bit. I would definitely recommend digging in when you have an opportunity and familiarizing yourself with Wireshark and the other protocol analyzer tools that are available. In this chapter, we covered vulnerability scan output. We talked about SIEM dashboards along with log files, such as syslog, rsyslog, and syslog-ng, how we can use those things to centralize our logging capabilities and then feed those in to other systems. We talked about journal control and some of the flags and some of the commands that can make that a useful tool for us along with an NXLog and then also retention of various types of things, like email and different types of data, and then the different types of compliance or regulations that may mandate that we retain certain types of data for certain periods of time. We also talked about bandwidth monitors and then metadata for various file types and how that can certainly divulge more information than we initially knew about. Then we talked about some network monitoring or optimization tools, such as NetFlow and sFlow, and then wrapped up with a brief look at protocol analyzers and protocol analyzer output.

Chapter 13 How to Implement Mitigation Techniques to Secure an Environment

In this chapter, we'll be talking about Implementing Mitigation Techniques to Secure an Environment. We'll be talking about reconfiguring endpoint security solutions, talking about application whitelisting and blacklisting, how that can help us, along with quarantining. We'll talk about configuration changes, and that deals with firewall rules, MDM, or mobile device management, data loss prevention, or DLP. We'll talk about content filters and also revoking and updating certificates. We'll also talk about the concepts of isolation, containment, and segmentation and how those can help us secure the environment, along with secure orchestration, automation, and response, or SOAR systems, and runbooks and playbooks specifically. When it comes to application whitelisting, that's going to be a list of applications that are allowed to run on a host. All other applications are blocked from running. That makes catching everything much easier. You don't have to know every single thing that could potentially run and explicitly deny that? In a whitelist, you say I have 10 applications that my users can run, Word, Excel, maybe a chat application, web browser of course, and a few other things. That's the 5 or 10 things you can do. That's all you can access. Everything else is blocked. Conversely, you can say blacklisting of an application, you can say, you know what, you can run everything except for these 5 or 10. All other applications are allowed to run. The downside being, if you have enough privileges you can go in and simply rename an executable that was previously blacklisted. As an example, you don't want someone to run regedit so they can't modify the registry. Well, if they have command prompt access or they can -click on regedit, they can browse to it, click on it, and rename it. They can rename that application and then simply run it at that point because it's checking against that file name. Depending upon how you're set up and what types of controls you have in place, it's important to check through these things all the way through, take the mindset of an end user, look at all the ways they can get around the controls you put in place, and make sure the things you have implemented function the way you intend them to.

Quarantine
One method that we can use to make sure that applications don't run, that we don't want malicious applications, malicious scripts, or hosts that perhaps aren't patched or don't meet our specifications before they enter the network, we can do something called quarantine. A quarantine is a

proactive blocking of access or the ability to run or execute applications. Hosts that don't meet certain criteria, perhaps they don't have a certain code level, firmware level, patch level, applications or processes that are flagged as suspicious or malicious, we can keep them from accessing the network. Depending upon how our infrastructure is set up, we can identify those machines when they first enter the network and then cordon them off into a DMZ, or a demilitarized zone or a screened subnet, at that point we can make sure that they get patched or updated or somehow remediated to meet our specifications, and then allow them onto the network. Another way of doing that is having applications, whether it be antimalware or antivirus, block applications before they're able to do anything. Popular antimalware applications like Malwarebytes or Windows Defender or Sophos, there's a lot of them out there, McAfee, etc. They can block suspicious activity and they can quarantine downloads, applications before they're allowed to run. Then when we're talking about whitelisting applications, we can also have an allow list. You can see here we can specify certain applications that are allowed to run so that way if the antimalware software blocks that for some reason, we can add it in into a whitelist, so that way the next time we run it, the antimalware software won't block that application. These things are potentially malicious, they're going to be malware, ransomware, cryptojacking software, they would automatically be quarantined because the antimalware software would identify this, whether it be through a signature or some type of heuristics. We can then choose to either keep them quarantined and not allow them to run, or you can check the specific ones that you want to run and it will bring it back to life, and allow you to run that application. Typically not recommended, but if you know for a fact that something is safe, you can go ahead and check it off and then allow it to run.

Firewalls

A firewall is designed to isolate one network from another. It can be hardware or it can be software based. It can be either. It can be a standalone device, or it can be an integrated device, integrated into some other equipment, in other words, routers or switches. Whether you're a small office or a home office, you may have a small Netgear, or a Linksys, or even a Cisco router that combines a lot of functionality together. It can have a firewall. It can do NAT or network address translation, and, of course, routing functionality, as well, perhaps even switching. It just depends on the size of the network, how specific you want to get. There are different devices that can perform very specific functions, or there are integrated devices that can perform a lot of different functions together. If we have a diagram of outside users outside of the firewall, and you see the firewall denoted by a brick wall. And, incidentally, the term firewall historically came from buildings that were built very close to one another, and in order to prevent fire from jumping from one building to another when they were very close together, think like row homes, for instance, they would build brick walls in between these different buildings to prevent that fire from jumping from one to the other. That brick wall would act as a firewall, to prevent fire from jumping from one building to the other. The same concept is carried, and that's why you typically see a firewall being illustrated as a brick wall. Firewalls are typically used to block or limit outside traffic from entering a network. Whether it's corporate, medium-sized office, small office, or a home office, they all serve pretty much the same types of functions. However, firewalls can also be placed internally, inside of a network, to segment one area from another. For instance, you may have a large corporate environment that has different areas that you don't necessarily want them to communicate, or they shouldn't communicate from one to the other very easily. You can punch holes in the firewall to allow traffic, but generally speaking, these things are cordoned off from one another. For instance, if you have a PCI secure zone, like, say you have a very large enterprise that has some typical day-to-day workers, and you may have an R&D department, you may have an accounting department, a finance department. PCI secure means it contains credit card information and some type of personally identifiable information, you want to have that information cordoned off from the rest of the network. The finance folks don't necessarily talk to the R&D, or maybe the graphics department, just to prevent internal browsing of those resources. A firewall can be put into place between those segments on your internal network as well. It's important to understand, hardware versus software, firewalls can either be hardware or software based. They can be standalone devices or integrated into other devices, like routers and switches. Even if it is a hardware-based solution, it's still going to contain software. You can't just run it on hardware by itself. There has to be some software running behind the scenes. You can drop it onto a server and have that server function providing firewall functionality, or it can be a separate standalone piece of hardware. However, that hardware is still going to contain software or firmware. What are some types of firewalls? Well, we have packet filtering firewalls, and packet filtering firewalls allow or block traffic based upon a specific port, HTTP traffic, as an example, web traffic. That typically comes in over port 80. FTP, or

File Transfer Protocol, that's generated on port 21. You can configure the firewall to allow web traffic but don't allow FTP traffic, or allow DNS but don't allow NetBIOS, or time lookups, or whatever the case might be. You can break it down by port by port by port and get very specific, get very granular. Doing it based just on port, there's not a lot of intelligence there. It just simply looks at the port, and then it will either allow or block the traffic at that point. Next, we have proxy firewalls. A proxy firewall's going to be dual-homed, which means is going to have two network interfaces, typically one on each network, or on separate networks. That's going to segment internal users from the outside world, and it can mask the IP address using something called NAT, or network address translation. That gives an added layer of security because the outside world won't know who's communicating. All they'll see is the address of the proxy firewall. The proxy can also cache requests to improve perceived speed. If you have multiple users, as an example, that are accessing the same website while the first person to access that website or that URL will go out and pull it down from the web or from whatever resource it's getting it from. Subsequent requests, as long as that information is still sitting in the cache on that proxy server, so the next user goes out to that same web resource. Instead of going out to the web, or out to whatever resource they're getting it from, they'll get it directly from the proxy server, from the cache. It gives the perception that things are faster and that your network is all of a sudden more responsive. The next type of firewall is something referred to as a stateful packet inspection firewall, or SPI. An SPI firewall examines the packets and keeps the packet table of every communication channel. In other words, it has more intelligence than a simple packet filtering firewall, and it does a deeper dive. It examines what's inside. SPI tracks the entire conversation, so it gives you an increased level of security because it only allows packets from known active connections. If someone's trying to spoof or jump in the middle of a connection or a conversation, an SPI firewall understands that, and they say, wait a minute, I don't know who this is from. I haven't seen this before. This is in the middle of a conversation. There's no initiation. There's no back and forth to establish that connection. This just came out of here, so I'm going to drop that. It drops the packet. It gives you that added layer of security. It's better than simple packet filtering, which only looks at the current packet. However, it's possible to attack by overloading that state table. As we go through all of these different types of routers and switches and pretty much any type of infrastructure or equipment in our network, just understand that nothing is foolproof. There's always going to be a way, and there's always going to be hackers that are trying to somehow penetrate that device, crash it, get elevated privileges. Nothing's foolproof. That's why we're all employed. When it comes to configuring our firewall, we have a couple options. We have firewalls that are built in to our operating systems like we have here in Windows 10. There are other firewalls that are standalone devices, there are ones that are software based, hardware based, like we've talked about before. They all operate in the same fashion. They all allow you to go in and either allow or deny, implicitly deny, explicitly deny, or allow, applications, ports, users, IP addresses. Let's take a look at this. On my Windows 10 Desktop here, I have Windows Firewall open, and this is the Advanced Security? If you go into Windows Firewall Advanced Security, you'll see a number of rules for Inbound Rules and also Outbound Rules, some Connection Security Rules, some Monitoring Rules, and you can monitor in real time, but for this demo, we're going to look at Inbound Rules, specifically around Remote Desktop.

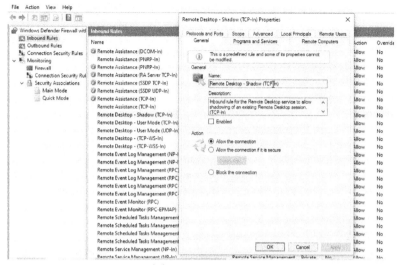

We want to enable Remote Desktop for this workstation. Conversely, if it was already enabled, and we think that might be a threat, we can disable that? Block that. So for here, if I double-click on any one of these, then I have a number of options. I can go in and look at the rule, the description, I can enable that rule, and if I hit Apply, you'll see the checkbox next to that rule. Programs and Services, there are some specific things around that application, Remote Computers. I can say, allow connections from these computers, or skip this rule for these computers. You can think of it as an application whitelist or a blacklist. Same thing for protocols and ports. I can go in and say remote ports, local ports. some of these things, depending upon what it is you're configuring, you may have to change port numbers within the registry, there might be some additional configuration that's needed, but the general gist is here. The Scope, I can say Local IP addresses, allow these IP addresses, or only these specific ones.

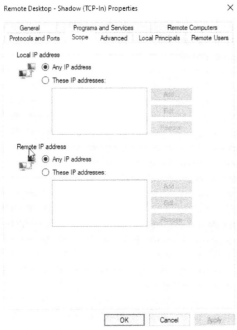

Same thing for Remote IP addresses. I can say Any IP address, or only allow these IP addresses. We're white-listing. Same thing for Advanced. I can say, which profile does this apply to? Is it Domain, is it Public or Private?

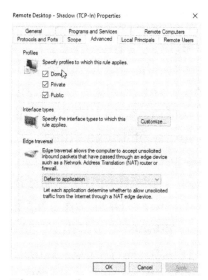

Then as far as Local Principals and Remote Users. I can say Local, only allow connections from these users, or skip this for these users?

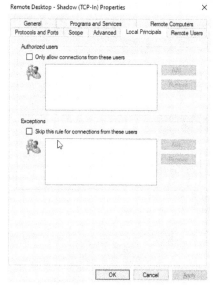

Again, white-listing and black-listing for Local users; same thing for remote. That's one way of doing it. I can go in manually, and you can also start from scratch and just say new rule, and create everything from scratch. If you have a specific application that might be brand new and you want to allow a certain port or a certain IP address, you can do that as well, or you can also configure some of these rules just by turning on, or turning off specific services. If I go and click on my Start button, and go up to System, then I'll see, at the bottom, Remote Desktop. This is one way to get to it. There's always more than one way to get to pretty much anything within Windows, but in this instance, I'm down at Remote Desktop.

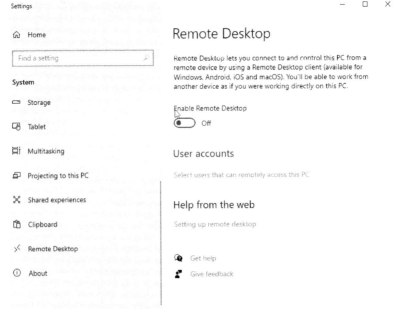

If I open that up and just turn on Enable Remote Desktop, it asks me, do you want to do this? I'm

going to confirm, Yes. And if I close that, and
Refresh, and I go back down to my Remote Desktop,
you'll see those three rules have been enabled.

Remote Desktop - Shadow (TCP-In)	Remote Desktop	All	Yes	Allow	No
Remote Desktop - User Mode (TCP-In)	Remote Desktop	All	Yes	Allow	No
Remote Desktop - User Mode (UDP-In)	Remote Desktop	All	Yes	Allow	No

The same thing I just did before manually, I did
automatically just by enabling Remote Desktop. If I
go back up, go to System, down to Remote Desktop,
and turn that off, I'm going to again, confirm I want
to Disable Remote Desktop. Refresh, go back down
again, and we see those three things are turned off.
Just an example of how to configure a firewall rule,
whether I want to allow or deny, based on port,
based on IP address, it could be based on user, or it
could be based upon application. There's more than
one way to do that. You can do it manually, as we
did here within the actual Management Console, or
I can do it automatically, just by turning on or
turning off certain features within the operating
system.

Chapter 14 Mobile Device Management

Mobile devices provide users with the flexibility, and they can access work from anywhere, access documents, pretty much anywhere on the planet, and they can conduct business as easily as they could if they're sitting in the office. But with any enterprise technology, security must be at the forefront. It's crucial that these things get vetted and thought through, and designed, and architected upfront with security in mind. We can't allow functions within the business to pick a solution, drop it on our lap. And then say, Hey, make this work. It happens, but if at all possible, we need to insert ourselves into the process far enough in advance so that's not the issue. Such things as insecure access to websites. If we don't make sure we have mobile device management in place, and we don't have some way of controlling what people use their corporate assets for, then they can access insecure websites, download malware, download viruses, data leakage. We have the insecure axis to websites, we have insecure Wi-Fi connectivity. If they're sitting in a coffee shop somewhere and they're accessing our corporate network, if we don't allow them VPN access or give them some secure method to do that, well, everything they type in, everything they browse on with that mobile device could be potentially sniffed from that device, and then company secrets, company proprietary information walks out the door. The other thing is lost or stolen devices housing corporate data. If someone sits at a coffee shop, we'll use that example, they lay their phone down on the table, they get up to go to the bathroom, they go up to pay for their drink or food or something, they turn around and the phone's gone. Well, if that device is not encrypted, there's a high probability that someone can pull that information off the phone very easily. Could be company secrets could be proprietary information, or if you don't have any way of locating that phone or remotely wiping it, there's no way for us to even tell where it is or if it's being used. There are a few things that should be put in place, and we'll talk about those more in detail in just a moment. But then again, geolocation services, if that phone gets lost or stolen, we should be able to figure out where it is. If that phone gets turned back on again and checks into the network, cellular network or Wi-Fi network, it should be able to phone home, and we should able to ping that device and see where it is; and then missing upgrades and security patches. If we don't have any mobile device management in place, we can't limit what they see, we can't make sure they secure their connections. We can't prevent it from being lost or stolen and having that data gone, we can't locate it on a map, and then we can't even make sure that the users install upgrades and security patches. mobile device management is critical on a number of levels to make sure that people are doing what they're supposed to be doing; unauthorized downloads, applications, games, and so on. With iOS devices, iPhones, it's a little easier because everything that goes through the app store meets certain criteria, so there's not as many rogue applications or things like viruses and Trojans, and back doors. On Android devices, their app store is a little more open. The platform is more open, so there's a greater opportunity to have applications or games that may be compromised, that may contain malware and viruses. With mobile device management, MDM software is what enables a company to secure that users BYO device, bring your own device, without compromising their personal information. Some MDM software can partition that phone, that "corporate asset" so that there is a partition that houses company data, and then the rest of it is the user's personal device. here's a couple of companies that can do that, I'm not recommending one over the other, I'm just giving you a couple examples: Good Messaging, Airwatch, and Mobile Iron are three very popular MDM companies that provide software that can allow you to do just that. Someone can bring their own phone, they install this MDM software, creates a separate partition, or it can create a separate partition on that phone, so that way the user can access company assets, company resources, but yet the company is not going to interfere or co mingle with their personal data. They can use it pretty much as a dual device. However previously, if the device gets lost or stolen, the company can at least wipe the corporate partition. They can make sure that any company data, any company secrets, so on can be wiped. They can remotely wipe the entire phone, they can geolocate it, they can require passwords, require patches, and security fixes are upgraded or downloaded and applied in a timely fashion. It gives much more control over that phone, and you can do it in such a way that it doesn't completely hamstring the user and turn that device into only a corporate device, they can use it as a dual purpose asset.

Using MDM to Locate and Secure and Lost Device
Now that we're clear on what MDM software is, the capabilities, let's talk about using this to secure a device, securing a lost device. But we have Alice, and Alice loses her phone, which has very important personal information, as well as corporate data. If Alice is anything like me when I lose my phone, I'm not very happy about it, and I panic quite a bit. Immediately, Alice turns around and calls her good friend, Bob, who happens to be the mobile device

management admin. Bob goes ahead and logs into his MDM console, brings up his tracking software, and is able to locate her phone. He's able to remotely access that phone via the MDM console over the internet. The phone's connected. It's turned on. He's able to access it. It's not somewhere they can readily get to the phone, so they make the decision to remotely wipe the phone. They issue a wipe command. It goes back to its default factory state. There's nothing on there. On the off chance that somebody comes by, let's say, Harry the hacker, and grabs that phone, there is no corporate data, there is no personal data. And that phone can be replaced, and the data is secure.

Chapter 15 DLP, Content Filters & URL Filters

Let's just set the stage here for a moment, and all of the things that we're talking about, we need to make sure that we can implement those things in the event of an incident. Let's just say, for argument's sake, that there's an incident that's happened at the company. It's been discovered that there have been several breach attempts over the last 4 to 6 weeks targeting financial systems, web servers, and potentially customer data. Malware has been discovered on numerous systems, several which have been found trying to connect to C2 or command and control servers, to download additional malicious software. Data exfiltration attempts have also been made using several techniques over common ports, and then reconnaissance-type activity has been observed, and it's currently unclear if corporate web servers have been compromised. Keeping that type of incident in mind, which is not an uncommon scenario, lots of companies have exactly those types of things happen, if not more, and a lot of times those things go undetected for months and months. The average breach is about 18 months, give or take, before it's detected. These things can happen in the background for quite a while. Some additional mitigation techniques that we can use, one will be data loss prevention, or DLP software. DLP software can mitigate data exfiltration, which is what we mentioned in the previous scenario. That data exfiltration can be blocked or that activity can be blocked by DLP software, anything that we deem suspicious. That can be blocked from many sources, whether it be web, email, removable devices, USB drives, as well as suspicious activity such as file access or suspicious user actions. Next, we have content filtering and URL filtering. Content filters and URL filters, we've talked about those before, but they can block access. We can cut that link so that the hosts cannot reach out to those command and control servers. That malicious site that they would typically connect to can download additional software, that link is broken. Whether it's downloading additional software, connecting to botnets, participating in distributed denial-of-service-attacks, all of those types of things can be stopped if we can do content filtering and URL filtering at our own location. Then even further up the food chain, those things can be stopped at the root and the top-level domain servers. Then it's possible to stop that activity at a much larger scale. Then also within our organization, we can update or revoke certificates. Expired or compromised certificates can allow attackers to falsify their identity, they can create trusted applications, steal data. We need to make sure that we revoke certificates, we publish it to a CRL, and those things are updated constantly. We need to make sure we update our browsers, patch when appropriate, as soon as possible, and also patch all the systems very, very quickly. It's also a matter of user training to make sure that users know not to click on expired certificates. If they get a warning that says, that certificate is expired, don't assume that it's just because, well, it was valid yesterday. It's expired today. Someone in IT probably just forgot to renew the certificate, so I'll just go ahead and click on it anyway. Make sure they understand it's all part of cybersecurity training and the culture of security, but make sure they understand that those things are not to be trusted. Trust no one. If you get an expired certificate warning, then take it to heart. Don't click on it. Don't engage in that activity.

Segregation, Segmentation and Isolation
Next, let's talk about segregation, segmentation, and isolation. We have a few security or segmentation models I want to call to your attention. First, is physical. We can physically separate or segment nodes or hosts on a network. We can also do that logically with something called VLAN, or virtual LANs, virtual local area networks. We can also do it with virtualization. It's an isolation model or a segmentation model. Then we also have air gapped, meaning there is no connectivity to the

internet or to the network at large. Well, with physical or logical, we have devices that are all on the same segment, the same Ethernet segment, or the same LAN, the same local area network, and in this example, you can assume that they're all connected to the same switch. That is a physical connectivity to the network. Well, we can also logically separate those networks. We can take that same layout, but we can use something called virtual LANs, or virtual local area networks, and group them accordingly. We could have a VLAN10, we could have a VLAN20, and a VLAN30. And what that does is separate those devices out. And what it does is create separate broadcast domains, separate security domains, and it reduces the chatter. Let's look at another example. Now we have a multi-floor building. We have wiring on each floor that goes back to a home run, and it goes down between floors. We have devices on the first floor and a switch, we have devices on the second floor and a switch, and then devices on the third floor and a switch. In this example, and it's not the only way to wire, not the only way to do it, but in this example we have each floor going to a wiring closet. In that wiring closet is a switch, and then the switches are connected via home runs. Vertical up and down wiring goes between floors, so they're all physically located in different locations. Well, we can also group those together, just like we did in the previous example. They don't have to be sitting next to each other. We can group them, again, logically, VLAN10, VLAN20, and then VLAN30. In other words, if we had groups of computers that may be on different floors. Let's say we have finance people that sit on all three floors or HR, or our graphics department, whatever the case might be, we can group them within our switches. We make sure that all the switches have the same VLAN associations, and that way they're grouped logically together. These VLANs can group hosts that are in different locations, into logical groupings. That creates smaller collision domains and reduces chatter. As an example, if you have a very large cafeteria, everyone's talking, it's very hard to understand because everyone's talking. Everyone's clashing into each other. They're colliding, their conversations. If I took all of those people in that cafeteria and separated them out into, say, five different rooms or, in this example, three different rooms, well, I have one third of the amount of people in each room, so the chatter's going to be less, so the collisions are less, so it helps increase efficiency. Then also it can be used to create security boundaries to segment traffic so that one host doesn't necessarily see broadcasts and doesn't see traffic designated for hosts in another VLAN.

Virtualization

Virtualization is the method of segmenting or isolating. We can keep a host in a sandboxed and isolated environment, meaning it's separate from the host that it's sitting on. It can also allow for snapshots. We can quickly revert changes, we can use virtualization to isolate our segment. We can do all of our testing. We can test changes we can even test viruses or malware to see what it does without affecting the rest of the network and without affecting the host that it sits on. It also separates the guests from the host, the guest from the hypervisor. If we have Hyper-V or VMware, or KVM, or VirtualBox, whatever our virtualization technology is, this allows us to keep those individual guests separate from the host. Other devices can be virtualized as well. We can virtualize other infrastructure, such as routers, switches, load balancers, firewalls. But the nice part is those things can be instantiated or spun up on demand. As a load increases, we could spin up additional load balancers or, if we have applications that need specific firewalls, instead of having to go through the normal change process and buying the equipment, and racking and stacking, and all the things that are associated with physical infrastructure, we can do it virtually very quickly, spin that device up, use it while we need it, and then we can tear it down just as quickly.

Air Gaps

An air gap is a method of isolating a computer or a network from the internet or from other external networks, or other networks aside from the one you're on. It doesn't necessarily have to be just from the internet. It could be from other networks within your company. If you have a very highly secure environment that you need to make sure that there's no chance of malware or viruses being introduced, then you would set up an air-gapped network. As with anything, there is no 100% guarantee, as we've seen in the past, with things like Stuxnet and some other very highly visible and highly cited instances where malware has jumped into air-gapped environments, nothing is 100% certain. But anyway, it's used for critical infrastructure, SCADA systems, as an example, and I refer back to Stuxnet, where the SCADA systems were still compromised, highly secure classified networks. There are some advanced techniques, however, to jump air-gapped networks. That's been demonstrated. Emanations, there's a technology, and it's been completely demonstrated, where they can view the emanations coming off of a computer, whether it is the sound of the hard drive whirring, or even the heat being generated by the hard drive spinning up. If you're close enough to that device, you can pick those things up from the device and discern what's going on. You can read data from that device, pretty scary stuff, pretty advanced stuff. It's not something the average hacker I can do. But just understand that an air gap is a very good way of isolating the network, but it's not 100% foolproof. In fact, the US government and other agencies around the world have specific guidelines to create additional security. The US uses something referred to as TEMPEST, which protects that room, has to be certain thickness of walls and has to have additional coating and protections, Faraday cages, and things that just prevent emanations and monitoring from nearby locations. Emanations, FM frequencies, even some hard drives that have a small LED light on the front that shows activity of that drive. You don't see that too much anymore, but it is possible that if you have a line of sight visibility to that light going on and off as the hard drive writes, you could read, almost like Morse code, what's going on with that hard drive and read data from that device.

Securing the Environment using Isolation, Containment and Segmentation
Now getting back to our previous example, and we're talking about this incident that occurred and how we want to secure the environment, we can use these three technologies and techniques to secure the environment. We need to make sure that we air gap a network. If we have automation in

place to create an air-gapped network, great. If not, and it's a manual procedure or we need to shut down ports, then, so be it. But if we're able to air gap that network, we can keep attackers out or keep compromised systems from spreading. There should be plans in place, and we'll talk about runbooks and playbooks here in just a moment, but there should be some things in place defined so that if and when an incident happens, we have the ability to isolate when possible or where possible, especially as I mentioned around our most critical environment or most critical assets. Next, containment. Virtualization can separate hosts from guests and also guests from each other. We can also use that technology to revert to an earlier snapshot. If we find that we're compromised, we can revert that machine back. We can clone systems as necessary, spin up additional systems or additional resources. We can also use that cloning technology to clone a system, take it offline, and then forensically investigate that system or do whatever investigations are necessary to help us track down what happened, where, when, why, how. Then also, segmentation. We can use VLAN technologies I talked about before to create separate subnets, separate logical subnets within our environment that help to mitigate the risk from ransomware, malware. By creating those logical separations, we can break the connections between the two. We can isolate or contain, if necessary, if we have VLANs set up or we can also very closely watch or tighten down our firewalls, tighten down our routers, and we only allow certain types of traffic through. We can allow critical things to allow business to operate, but not necessarily everything through. We can ratchet that down or turn it up as necessary. All of these technologies can help us secure an environment in the event of a breach and also proactively if we suspect something may be happening.

SOAR and Runbooks/Playbooks

Next, we have something referred to as SOAR, and that stands for Security Orchestration, Automation and Response. What this does is complement your SIEM software. They do have some overlapping capabilities, but it complements SIEM software versus replacing it. It's going to allow us to aggregate all of the tools within a SOC, or security operations center, and then provides automated playbooks. We can script a lot of these actions together, not just within our SIEM software, but it may also kick off ticket creation, case management. It also has integration with third-party products. There's numerous things that it can integrate with, and then it automates, it orchestrates and automates that response. The SIEM software will collect all this data, it'll generate alerts, it'll do all of its things. It can bring in other sources to help enrich that data, and then it can help kick off investigations, open cases, open tickets, take remediation steps. It provides a full toolbox of capabilities. Imagine if we have a SOAR platform that sits in the middle. We're going to have different things on the left here. Events are coming in, our SIEM software, our endpoint detection, endpoint detection and response software is all going to be generating information and data. All of that stuff can then be fed into the SOAR platform, which can then do other things like ticketing, IT ticketing, change control, and it can also integrate with other controls, alerting, whitelisting applications or whitelisting protocols, and then also are third-party tools. You can think of it as the glue that holds a number of different applications and capabilities together and allows them to talk and integrate with each other, orchestrating and automating that interconnectivity. Getting back to the earlier incident, we've experienced some incident, and we need to have these different tools and technologies to help us secure the environment. We can leverage the SOAR platform to help us with orchestration and automation, the whole point of the platform. But these things are all predicated on us having very clearly-defined runbooks and playbooks so that we understand what needs to happen, in what order it needs to happen, who needs to be alerted. Let's take a look at this in a little more detail. These runbooks and playbooks, and this is just an example, this is not an exhaustive list, but some things that need to be defined and then put into the SOAR platform where possible to help us automate some of these actions. What tickets are to be created? What changes need to be implemented and also in what order? Depending upon the size of the environment, you may have a very complicated or a very wide-reaching change management system. A lot of different systems that are integrated, some things feed other things. You might be a 24/7 organization. You might have a lot of public-facing customers. You might be mandated by certain regulations and compliance mechanisms. All of these things have to be carefully vetted and also orchestrated so that they happen as quickly as possible, but without creating additional disruption to the business. What tickets need to be created? What changes have to be implemented? And in what order is critical. Also, what teams need to be engaged? What management teams need to be alerted and when? Also, what additional resources should be added? Whether that be monitoring resources. Do we need to spin a site up? Do we already have a site? Are we in the cloud and we need to spin up additional resources? Also callouts; do we have additional resources, vendors, third-party labor that needs to be engaged, also vendor engagements? Most of these systems are provided by some type of vendor, we should engage them as well to get their subject matter experts on task as quickly as possible. And then some additional items that should be defined, network changes. Are we going to look at isolation or containment or segmentation? Some of these things can be automated. Are we going to be taking clones or reverting from snapshots? Again, failing over to a remote site or up to the cloud. Do we have a dark IP space that's air gapped that we can move things over into or we may have been synchronizing with? Our most critical systems may have been synchronizing in the background and then logically air gapped. Well, do we need to spin up that dark IP site and revert to a last-known good configuration, or a last-known good set of data? Then from an investigation standpoint, spinning up investigations, who do we contact? What types of things do we preserve? Do we need forensics in place? Is there a preservation of evidence or a chain of custody that needs to be maintained? All of these things should be defined ahead of time. We don't want to be flushing these things out in the middle of a breach or in the middle of an incident. The more planning we have in place ahead of time, the more documentation that we have, and that everyone knows what the roles and responsibilities are, and then the runbooks and playbooks can then run that much more efficiently. We can automate where possible. The SOAR platform, this orchestration and automation is a big piece of this puzzle. It's the glue that holds all of these things together. The more planning we do ahead of time, the more successful the outcome. In this chapter, we talked about reconfiguring endpoint security solutions like application whitelisting and blacklisting. We talked about quarantining, whether it be applications or processes or downloads and. We talked about configuration changes like firewall rules, MDM, wiping devices remotely, DLP. We talked about content filters and also revoking or updating certificates. We also talked about isolation, containment, and segmentation and how that can help us secure the environment. Then we talked about SOAR, which is Secure Orchestration, Automation and Response, along with runbooks and playbooks and how those things will help us be successful in the event of an incident.

Chapter 16 Key Aspects of Digital Forensics

In this chapter we'll be talking about Understanding the Key Aspects of Digital Forensics. We'll talk about documentation and evidence in general and why it's Very important to make sure things are documented properly. We'll talk about acquisition and some things around what we should go after first and why, some of the gotchas if we don't follow those procedures. We'll talk about integrity and a few methods we can use to prove that the data we've collected has not been tampered with. We'll talk about preservation along the same lines. We'll talk about ediscovery and what that means and how it applies to an investigation, along with data recovery, and then a similar concept of nonrepudiation so the party in question can't deny ownership or specific action. And then we'll talk about strategic intelligence and counterintelligence along with on-prem versus cloud and some of the challenges and nuances to where that data resides, some things around data sovereignty, applicable laws, depending upon where it's located in the country or in the world if we're doing global business. But what is computer forensics? Well, it is the analysis of digital data in a very simple term. A forensics-level investigation would be something a lot more sophisticated and typically a lot deeper than simply just logging into someone's computer and reading through their internet cache or their internet history. The mere fact that we log in to someone's computer and try to check those things, we tamper with that data. It renders the investigative process, or the probative value, it renders it more or less useless. We have to make sure that we do it when we do investigations in a very controlled, predetermined fashion so that we don't either knowingly or unknowingly tamper with or contaminate the evidence that we're trying to preserve. It's an analysis of digital data, and that can be computers, it can be smartphones, USB drives, it can be the internet activity taking place, text messages between two people or groups, game consoles, and more. Everything that's connected to the internet, even the Internet of Things, whether it's a refrigerator or, all of those things generate information. They generate data that can be used to either put someone at the scene of a crime or at least help to corroborate a chain of events. Who uses computer forensics? But, anyone who has a need to gather and retain digital evidence. Anyone, whether it's a small mom and pop shop and they may hire a third party to come in and do that, a criminal or computer forensics investigation, or it can be a very large company, a corporate enterprise, a Fortune 500 or a Fortune 150 global organization, they may have an entire team of forensic investigators that they can either dispatch anywhere around the world or they can work remotely anywhere in the world. A small business investigating an internal data breach, a large corporation investigating a hacking attempt or data theft, so anyone from small to the very large has a need for computer forensics. Also, law enforcement investigating a crime. It doesn't necessarily have to be an internal group or department within a company, law enforcement oftentimes will do some type of computer forensic examination, and that's becoming more and more prevalent as time goes on. 10 - 15 years ago it was relatively unheard of to have each department have a specific computer forensics lab or a computer forensics division. Nowadays, pretty much every department has either one or two, or maybe an entire department devoted to computer crime investigation and computer forensics. Additionally, we have private detectives, investigating spouses and insurance fraud.

Order of Volatility
Computer evidence is stored in a number of locations. It can be stored on a magnetic disk, it can be stored in a flash, it can be stored in RAM. Some locations are very temporary. RAM, or random-access memory, is one of those. Everything that your computer does, when it interacts, the

CPU, or the brains of your computer or your smartphone or your game console or whatever it is, all of those things have a CPU of some sort. That CPU cannot communicate directly with the data on disk or the data on a flash drive or what have you. It has to pull that data into RAM. That's the intermediary, or the staging area. That is the place where the CPU talks to when it needs to do something of a process. The information in RAM is fresh, it goes in and out very quickly. There's only a finite amount of RAM, and things that come into RAM, if it's already full then it will cache out or swap out or page out, depending upon the operating system that you're using. It'll take that data out of RAM and place it on the disk. Well, that RAM can go away very quickly if the computer is turned off or if it loses power. That's one thing we have to be aware of. Some locations are longer term, Even after deletion that information or that data remains. Magnetic hard disks are a good example of that. If you delete a file from a disk, in other words you just simply highlight it and then click Delete, that file is not deleted. What it is is it takes off the master file table, or again, or it depends upon the operating system how that functions, but there's some table of contents, that has all the pointers to where those files are located. When you delete a file you simply remove that marker. You ultimately say, hey this file is capable or able to be over written. This location of data is no longer needed. It takes the pointer away, so it makes it look like the file is no longer there, but the data itself remains until it's overwritten. This pertains to hard disks. Flash drives are a little bit different. But for magnetic hard disk, if you delete something it doesn't go away. Some locations, are long term, but once deleted they quickly become irretrievable. This specifically refers to SSD or flash drives. With magnetic disks we can place our 1s and 0s, or our bits on the disk. And if we erase that or we mark it for deletion those bits remain. With an SSD, you can't overwrite information in an SSD. If I have information there and I mark that file for deletion I can't simply just overwrite it because it can only have two states, on or off, it's a flash drive. I need to erase that and set it back to 0s so that it can then be over written. When that happens I'll mark the file for deletion, and then very quickly behind the scenes there's a trim process or a garbage cleanup function that takes place and it will then clear that data out. Once you delete it off an SSD, sometimes within minutes, sometimes within half an hour or an hour, depending upon the type of flash drive and what functionality it has, that data will be deleted and it's irretrievable. From a forensics perspective, where that data is stored has some type of bearing on how quickly you need to access it and the order in which you should access it. With the order of volatility, data should be gathered based on the life expectancy of that data. The CPU, cache, and register content, okay the things that are closest to the CPU that need to be there, or need to have power there for it to exist and continue to exist, that is the top of the priority list. We want to try to capture that information first because that information, most often than not or more often than not, will have the most probative value. But it's also the easiest to disappear. If we turn the computer off that information is gone. Next, we have the routing tables, ARP cache, process table, kernel statistics, again, all things that are very volatile. Memory, RAM, all of these things, temporary file space, swap space, data on hard disk, remotely logged data, data contained on archival media. It goes from the things that are very ephemeral, where if we power that computer off it goes away. Those things need to be captured, if at all possible, first. There are tools we can hook up to a computer, we can attach either locally or remotely that allow us to capture that data without contaminating it. Then we can do the same thing with routing table, ARP cache, and memory. The remaining things, temporary file systems, swap space, we can capture that because it's written to disk and the data on the hard disk. We can do that in a slightly more methodical, deterministic fashion. With the data in that volatile space, memory and

RAM, that's a little more difficult to capture, but it also provides, a lot of times, the most value because it shows us exactly what was happening just within a few moments ago.

Chapter 17 Chain of Custody & Legal Hold

There's something that can be critical to an investigation, and it can also sink an investigation. Even if it's the best, most meticulously conducted investigation on the planet, if it fails during the chain of custody, if and when it ever has to go to court, that could sink the investigation. When collecting evidence, maintaining that chain of custody is crucial. We want to make sure that we have no gaps in the chain of custody because why? Well, because that can destroy a case. If in other words, if there's a gap and we collect all of our evidence, we do all of our due diligence, we get our search warrant, we go in and we take possession of equipment, we document, and do all the things that we're supposed to do, but then we bring that back to our headquarters or to our office, and we don't document where that evidence goes, whose hands it changes along the way, where it's stored, and so on, it's very easy for a defense attorney, at that point, to interject and say, well, wait a minute. How do we know this wasn't tampered with during the process? How do we know that this wasn't swapped out or something wasn't manipulated or tainted in some fashion? There's hours, there's days, there's weeks where no one had eyes on this specific equipment. How do we know this is even my client's computer or hard drive? You don't want to have that discrepancy come into the investigative process. Evidence can become contaminated, if we don't have it accounted for each and every step of the way. It also introduces reasonable doubt. The defense attorney can turn the tables on an investigation. It's important to lock this thing down tightly and do not leave any room or any chance for error. When we're dealing with custody logs, it should accompany each piece of evidence. Everything that we secure, everything that we take away from a scene, should have a chain of custody tag attached to it, an evidence tag, depending on how your specific department or organization works. That chain of custody tag should have who acquired it, who received it or who it was received from, the date, and the time. That should account for everything, including when it's logged into an evidence locker, when it's removed from an evidence locker, so, there is no gaps in time. Every time the evidence is logged in or out of evidence or an evidence locker or some type of containment facility or changes hands in any form, that should be documented, the date, the time, the location, the person checking it in, checking it out, and then seals and/or tags on evidence bags. If an evidence bag needs to be opened, then it should be written on there why that seal is broken and when a new seal is applied, and, of course, initialed. That way everything is accounted for from the moment it is acquired to the moment it's no longer needed.

Legal Hold
Legal holds is data that has been identified as material to an investigation. It's copied or moved to an immutable location. Immutable means it can't be altered in any way. That way it's write protected, so that way it helps us maintain a continuity of evidence. there are different applications out there that will do a lot of this for us, so all actions, access, anything that's done to that data, if anyone accesses it, moves it, uses it in any type of searches, all those things will be logged. There are a number of applications and application suites or tool sets that will do all of that for us and automate a lot of this process. Something else to keep in mind is the fact that it's not subject to typical retention policies, so it may in fact be held indefinitely. Your organization may have, say, a 30-day, or a 3-month, or even a 3-year data retention policy, or 5 or 7 years, depending upon the type of data. Well, legal hold data will be held indefinitely until that specific case is over, and in some instances, that data may be held indefinitely. Some companies may keep that data in an immutable location on a higher class of storage or a higher tier of storage while the case is active, and then archive that off to something else, whether it be DVD or some write-once media, or it

might move to tape backup or some type of archive location, so that way it can be held indefinitely but then recalled, if need be, whether it's part of its own case, or it may be part of some other case.

Chapter 18 First Responder Best Practices

The first responder can be on scene, or you can image your computer remotely over a network, again, depending upon the role that you play, whether you're law enforcement or an internal corporate investigator, whether you work for a state or a local, or the federal government. Each of these different tiers, have different capabilities. Once you're there, you need to photograph the computer, photograph the scene. It's critical to get a good understanding of how things are, again, if you're local to that scene, if you're not doing it remotely. If you're on scene, photograph the computer and the scene. That way, you know exactly from beginning how things are laid out, how things are connected. Then if the computer is off, do not turn it on. The simple act of you turning on a computer and booting it up changes thousands of files, changes the timestamps, the last access, last modified on a number of files, hundreds of thousands of files, just simply booting the operating system. That can have a negative effect on your investigation. It can wipe out some things that could be extremely valuable down the road. It's off, don't turn it on. Then if it's on, don't turn it off, at least not yet. We want to photograph the scene, make sure we have everything in place. Then, if you have the proper tools, again, you can connect to that computer, whether it's USB, whether it's some other type of method, and you can image, you can write block the computer, and then image it without contaminating anything. You can capture the information that's in RAM, that's in all the volatile areas that we talked about in addition to imaging the actual disk itself. That way you can get an exact duplicate of the data that's on that computer and the state that it's in when you come across it. You want to turn off if you have the tools available to do that type of imaging. Then, depending upon your role, whether it's IT security or whether you're law enforcement, will dictate whether you can or can't put your hands on someone, if you're law enforcement and you're doing the search warrant, you want to make sure you separate that person from the device. Because if they have the chance to get to the computer, start erasing files, turning it off, or doing something to manipulate the device. In some instances, there have been cases where people have their computers hooked up to explosives, they have degaussing coils, so if they flick a switch they can turn around and wipe their hard drive instantly. Some extreme cases, but depending upon your role, you want to separate the person and the computer, image it on site. That's not always possible, but these types of things are best practices that allow you to get with the least chance of contamination the data that you need in a format that will stand up and hold up in a court of law, if it ever has to go through an investigative process and it ends up in court. I don't want to get off on a tangent too, too much, but, again, you'll separate the person, then you'll collect live data. You want to start with the RAM image. You want to get all that data that you can off the computer in its live, volatile format so that you can look at and parse through what that person was doing at that exact point in time. Because if they just had a chat conversation with someone, or if they were just logging into a website, doing some type of hack or a breach, the things that they typed most recently in that conversation, the data that's passed through the computer will be stored in RAM. That gives you a high-value target. Then you want to collect a local image of the hard disk using forensics tools, and there are many tools out there, so this is not an endorsement of any one product. But there are tools like dd, Helix3, EnCase, F-Response. There's a number of tool. AccessData is another. There are a lot of ones out there that can give you a forensic bit-by-bit copy of a hard drive without writing to that drive at all. Takes an exact copy, bit-level copy, creates a hash against that copy, so it does a hash on the original, does a hash on the copy, and those hashes will match up. It gives you the ability to say definitively, yes, that's exactly the same data as what was retrieved or what existed on the suspect computer. Once that's finished, then you can unplug in the power cord from the back of the computer or remove the battery. The power cord is the best way to go, or removing the battery. There have been instances where the power button has been wired to a degaussing coil or some type of explosive, in some cases. If you flick that power button, you have the potential to not get the desired result. So removing the power cord, removing the battery if it's a laptop, is the best option. That way it shuts it down ungracefully, doesn't write to the swap file, any of those things. It just shuts it off at the point in time that it was. Then once we're done, we want to diagram and label all cords, document all devices themselves, model numbers, serial numbers. That part of an investigation is very time consuming. It's certainly not the most glorified part of the investigation, but it is critical because all of those things need to be documented properly, so they can be reconstructed, if necessary, or at least very accurately describe the scene as you found it.

Capture a System Image

A system image can be captured locally or remotely using special software or devices. There are applications that can do it via software, but there are also other applications or devices that can do it through a hardware connectivity. It will write-block the computer or the device in question, and when I say write-block, you're not able to write to that disk at much like read-only, but better. That way, even if it's read-only, there are still some things that could be accessed just by the nature of you interacting with the file system. When you write-block the computer, you literally turn off its ability to write at all. That way you can image that disk, you can create a forensic image, a bit-level, bit-by-bit image of that disk, even the slack spaces on the drive, is then copied to a duplicate. When you're done, you would run a hash, and if the hashes match up, you know it is an exact duplicate of the suspect device or the suspect file, folder, disk. There are live USB or CD/DVDs, whatever your media of choice is, and when I say live, what I mean is that these are ISO images that are on the USB or a CD or a DVD. That computer will boot up, but it boots up completely off of the USB drive or the CD. Nothing is written on the hard disk, and there are a number of devices out there. Kali Linux is one but there are literally dozens of different distributions and programs from encase, access data, and there's lots of them out there that can give you these live, bootable images that can give you forensic capabilities on a target PC, laptop, etc. Something else to keep in mind when talking about capturing a system image is to make multiple copies of the imaged data. The reason for that is that we want to make sure we have a copy that we're working off of, never the original data. We don't want to work on the original image or the original PC or laptop, simply because, that will contaminate the data. We make multiple copies; that way, we can work off of a copy if something goes wrong, or we need to in some way destroy it or go through some type of destructive analysis, we can always go back and start with a new or a fresh image to copy the next time we have to do something again. That way, we're always working off of a copy that we can verify via that hashing algorithm. We can verify it is an exact duplicate of the original. We never want to use the actual target hard drive, simply because it contaminates the data. Forensic software will log and timestamp every action that we take during the investigation. That way, we can build what's called a case folder to aid in the documentation and the reporting, because if we're simply trying to determine what happened, if it's a breach, if it's someone that's trying to hack into our system, we may never have any desire to take this to court, or we know it's not going to go anywhere from a legal standpoint, but we want to understand what happened, how we can harden our defenses. In that case, it's not as important. But if we're talking about a criminal case where we think, or there has the potential for that case to go to court at some point in time, it is crucial that we maintain proper evidentiary procedures, and making sure we maintain chain of custody. But having that documentation again is critical, because it's very important if it ever goes to court, we want to make sure that we can recall that testimony and make sure that we can understand, very systematically what we did, and it may be six months, a year, two years down the road before that goes to court. If we're not aware of what we did, we don't have a photographic memory, that documentation is going to be extremely important.

Chapter 19 Network Traffic and Logs

The next thing that you want to look at, or a potential for digital evidence would be network traffic and logs. If you think about it, every single thing that's attached, whether it be a local network, a small office, home office network or a SOHO, SMB, small- to medium-sized business, or a corporate enterprise, again, a Fortune 500 or Fortune 150, every single device that's connected in any fashion generates logs, generates traffic. Network traffic, including IP addresses, the data that sent, the actual websites we're browsing or the photos that we're accessing, the data that we're either copying or saving, the protocols that we use, all can be used to investigate a crime or a hacking event. An IP address, for example, can be used to locate the source and the destination of an event. It can help us to narrow down where a suspect is located. It could be on our internal network. We could be in a corporate environment trying to identify who a suspect is, who's accessing files. It doesn't necessarily mean that we know exactly who that person is because, again, someone could be sitting at that person's computer. Same thing if we're investigating a crime from a law enforcement perspective as well. Just because we have someone's IP address doesn't necessarily mean we know exactly who that person is. That gives us an idea, that gives us a start, but that only begins the actual investigative process. Once we have the IP address we can narrow it down, we can potentially see where they're coming from, what, perhaps, hops they're taking to get from where they're located to their destination. They may be trying to hide where they're located, we can backtrack and see if that leads us to the end, or to the suspect, rather. Sometimes it will go to a dead end, if they're smart enough and they jump through enough hoops. It doesn't necessarily always mean we have a person of interest. It can help place the suspect behind the keyboard, but, that's just a piece of the puzzle. We have to have more than just that. Then logs themselves are generated by a variety of devices. If you think about desktops and laptops, there's lots of logs within the actual computers themselves as to what they're doing, when they're doing it, the registry on a PC, there's configuration files on Macs and Linux devices, lots of log files that are generated and saved, typically for troubleshooting. But it also identifies when files were accessed, when system parameters and variables were changed, when people logged on, or when they logged off. All of these things can help us to build a case. Routers, switches, and firewalls on our corporate network, or even if it's in a home and we're trying to identify what's taken place from my location to a corporate location. In other words, someone's outside of our corporate network and trying to come in. Routers, switches, and firewalls, both within our own environment and potentially within a suspect environment, can all create log files, syslog files on routers, switches, the firewalls themselves. All of these things should be gathered and then correlated. Once we have all this information, we then need some way of either feeding it into a big data analysis type of tool, something like Splunk or some type of other big data analysis tool so we can correlate all of these different pieces of information, log files from here, switch files from here, configuration files from here, and put them all together. Then we can correlate the times and get an idea of what's going on. Smartphones, gaming consoles, some other things that people typically don't think of, but, they all generate logs. Smartphones have diagnostic information. We can tell when it was used, what was installed. Gaming consoles, whether it be an Xbox or a PS3 or PS4, all of these things get IP addresses that they connect to the internet. They generate log files and generate data. Everything, if you take it and put it into a combined case folder, can lead to a pretty precise picture of what happened and when.

Capturing Video

Video can be a crucial component to documenting an investigation. It can be taken of ourselves or of yourself as you're in your investigation, You can wear a camera to record your movements or you can simply just video the scene itself you have a good picture of how things were laid out, where they are, record what's on the screen, the position, the location of various components, and so on. Also, video can be from a surveillance camera, whether it be on site or perhaps outside of a business or a specific data center or a location. Do we have evidentiary value or do we have evidence from video cameras inside of our data center about an office or a remote site, the entrance or an exit of a building. Video can be something that we take or it can be taken from an outside, third-party source that we can then use to help build our case. Video can be used in a number of different fashions.

Record Time Offset

When I talk about recording the time offset you might say, well why is that important? Who cares? Well, it's extremely important when we're trying to corroborate and correlate all these different log files that we have. There's something referred to as UTC. That stands for Coordinated Universal Time. It stands for Coordinated Universal Time. It's the mean solar time at the Earth's prime meridian. 0 degrees longitude located near Greenwich, England.

The time zones from around the world are expressed as positive or negative offsets from the UTC. Why that's important? Well, we may have people, whether they're suspects or even within our own corporation or our own corporate networks, that are global. Or they may be at least within different time zones. If we don't have the proper offset and we're not sure that everything is in sync then it's going to be very hard to try to build a case based on time. We could have multiple breaches within a corporate network, that take place across multiple time zones. It could be globally. If we're not able to correlate exactly what happened when it's going to be very difficult for us to then match up, Person A, our suspect, was at their location here and they hit our PC or our network here. Well if the times are completely offset and they're not accurate it's going to be much more difficult for us to lineup than if we can see that on the suspect computer at exactly 15:15 it did this, and here it is 15:15 on our systems as well and here's where the breach occurred. It's going to be much more difficult if everything is out of whack to try to correlate that. It's just, it's important for us to make sure that within our own systems that we have control over that we have all of our systems in sync pointing to a network time server. Okay? They can either be internal or it can be external. We can point our devices, routers, switches, PCs, we can point them to an external time source so that way everything is in sync. Typically in most environments, whether it's, a Linux environment or an Active Directory environment, more than likely you'll have the Active Directory server or, some component within your Active Directory environment, point to a time server. They will coordinate time and push out the proper time for all the computers within that environment. However, your switches and everything else, routers, they need to be in sync as well. That way it's very easy to corroborate and correlate time.

Taking Hashes

When we're talking about hashes, a hash can be an MD5, SHA1, SHA256 or SHA512, it's a mathematical algorithm that's applied to a file folder or an entire disk that verifies the integrity of the evidence. The hash is taken prior to imaging. If we arrive on scene and we take possession of a suspect computer, we have a device we can either connect externally or we boot up using some type of write-blocking software, we're going to connect to that target PC locally or remotely. We will then run a hash against that target hard disk, typically it's going to be the entire hard disk. We'll run a hash against it. It will come back when it's finished and spit out a number, a long string of characters and numbers telling us this is a unique fingerprint for that specific drive.

When we're done, we'll then take an image of that hard disk and we'll run that same hashing algorithm against the copy. If both of those numbers come back the same, we know beyond a shadow of a doubt that they are absolutely identical. If one letter, as an example, if we were to hash an entire dictionary or an entire encyclopedia or the entire Library of Congress, whatever it is you want to focus on, if you took a hash of that entire body of work, let's just say a dictionary, well, if we changed one letter in that dictionary from a lowercase to an uppercase, the hash would be completely different. In other words, if we were to make the analogy to a computer, if we went to a computer and just simply turned it on, accessed some files, logged in, things are going to change, timestamps, file access, whether we're read, write, modify, anything that we do at that point to that computer changes something. When that happens, it would then change the hash, and if those hashes are different between our target and our copy, well, then it's no longer valid, and in a court of law that would be thrown out.

Chapter 20 Screenshots & Witnesses

A screenshot of what is on a suspect's computer, on their screen at that moment in time, gives us an idea or a good indication of what they were doing, what they were working on, perhaps before they had a chance to destroy evidence. especially if we don't have the opportunity for the tools to take a proper image and grab what was in RAM and volatile memory, if we don't have the ability to capture that information, then our second best option is to take screenshots., again, we don't want to interact with the actual computer itself. If we have no other choice than yes, something is better than nothing; however, remember back to what I said if we have to go to a court of law and it depends upon the type of investigation, but we don't want to tamper with the original suspect PC if we can help it, but if you can't then taking screenshots can help. An alternative would be, either video or to take pictures and physically take a picture of what's on the screen at that point in time. Depending on what's on the screen, it may outweigh the risk, losing that information.

Witnesses
Something else that we want to not overlook for sure are witnesses. Witnesses and witness accounts

can be crucial to an investigation, and more often than not, a witness can help or kick off an investigation. A lot of times crimes, attempted crimes, breaches have been solved by tips from witnesses from the general public. Don't overlook the fact that there are always a second set of eyes, that can be crucial to your investigation. When taking statements from a witness, always try to ascertain the general who, what, where, why, and how, but also the date and time, what else was going on at that point in time, who else was there, because you may be able to have follow up witnesses. Maybe that person that you initially talked to didn't see everything or they weren't there long enough, but if they can also say who else was in the room or who else was in the general area and you're able to contact those people, you maybe able to get additional information as well. Also, what other equipment was present, because that may give you more things that you want to search, especially if you're going to prepare a search warrant and you want to make sure you include everything in your search warrant, but you don't want to be overly broad because as you take things before a judge, if it's overly broad, a lot of times they will shoot that down and make you go back and rework that search warrant you're wasting valuable time depending upon the nature of the crime. If you can pinpoint it, narrow it down, and get it the first time, then that's going to expedite your ability to get that warrant and go and get that evidence and then, you want to make sure you capture the who, what, where, when, why, and how. But if you capture all of these things and you touch all of these points when you're doing your interview, you're going to capture the majority of information that you need.

Chapter 21 Preservation of Evidence

As an example, let's say we have our target system. We have a couple of options. We could attach to it with a laptop and we could use software where I protect that computer. We could also use a USB or bootable disk we could boot into that system and boot to that live CD instead of allowing the system itself to boot. Because if you recall, the actual act of booting that system changes hundreds, potentially thousands of system files, access times, dates, so it tampers with that evidence. We want to use something, some device to write-protect that target system so that it's not tampered with. Alternatively, we could use some type of hardware or software device to connect, a USB token or a specific, or an actual device specifically built for forensic purposes that allows us to attach to that machine via USB or some other connection, and write-protect that system, and from there we would take a bit-level copy and we would create, in essence, a cloned image. Typically we'd take that bit-level copy, that entire computer, and copy it to an image file. That image file is then what we would work from. We would then take our forensics workstation, and we would work from that cloned image, we would not work on the actual target system. We can use a hashing algorithm to hash the original system and then hash our cloned working copy or copies and make sure they are identical. That way we can prove that nothing's been tampered with or have been added or changed in any way. But we always want to work off of an image. That way the original target system is preserved.

Recovery

When it comes to recovery from a forensics' perspective, data can be recovered forensically if it hasn't been overwritten. That's it at the end of the day. If the data has not been overwritten, it can be recovered using forensics tools. If it's been wiped, in other words it's been overwritten by multiple passes, that's going to make it very difficult, if not impossible, to have that data recoverable. If it's an SSD, if those NANDs have been reset, there are some tools, both from the SSD manufacturers and also some Linux tools from third-party tools that allow us to reset those SSDs so you can wipe that entire drive in a matter of seconds. If that, in fact, happens, recovery of that data is very, very difficult, if not impossible. Additionally, the media itself needs to be intact. If someone were to take a drill and drill through those hard drives or drill through the SSDs or otherwise break them apart, degauss them if it's a magnetic media, something where it physically destroys that disk, it's going to be very difficult, again if not impossible, to recover the data.

Depending upon what it is, the nature of the investigation, and who's doing the recovery, impossible is a relative term. There are some Three Letter Agencies that have access to tools and toolsets that the average person and the average company does not have. Impossible is not necessarily a finite term, but for all intents and purposes for the average company, for the average person doing forensics recovery, if the media is physically damaged, broken apart, drilled through, scratched beyond repair, that data is going to be unrecoverable.

Strategic Intelligence / Counterintelligence Gathering

Whether we're talking about strategic intelligence or counterintelligence, it's done to allow the person or the company commissioning those actions to make real-time, actionable decisions. The actions are going to be proactive based on real-time data. We're not looking at historicals, we're not looking at trends, this is real-time data, it's very fluid, it's real-time analytics, active logging activities that will typically have clearly defined rules of engagement and allow us to make very quick decisions based upon real-time data. Next, it relies on human interaction, as well as automated methods. Human reconnaissance or boots on the ground, as well as active logging and automated toolsets to gather that intelligence. We're not looking at logs and looking back historically, we're not looking in the rear view mirror, and we're looking at real time and looking forward to make these actionable decisions on how to act proactively. Then it can also be either defensive, which is our intelligence gathering, or offensive, which is counterintelligence. Intelligence information can be used to defend a company's or a country's interests or they can be offensive, and that's done to neutralize an adversary or an adversary's intelligence gathering capabilities. The mandate of most counterintelligence agencies are to go out and actively pursue, actively neutralize, or try to neutralize, an adversary's intelligence gathering capabilities. We're trying to thwart their ability to perform espionage, exfiltrate data from us.

Chapter 22 Data Integrity

Data integrity is part of the CIA triad, confidentiality, integrity, and availability, but with regard to digital forensics, just a few things to clarify. With data integrity, we have a couple of ways to provide data integrity, one of which is hashing. And as we know, hashing is a mathematical algorithm that maps data of an arbitrary size. It can be a variable, it could be short, it could be long, to a hashed value of a fixed size. It's pretty much deterministic. Every time we do a hash of a specific piece of information, we're always going to get the same result. It's a one-way function that's infeasible to reverse or inverse. There are a few different hashing algorithms, MD5, various flavors of SHA, SHA-1, SHA-256. So from a forensics perspective, you can hash the files on a drive and get a specific value. Then when you're done, when you've done your investigations or if you have a copy of that data, you can run that hash algorithm again. If those two hashes match, that means that the data has not been altered in any way. Next will be checksums. It's very similar in functionality to hashes as far as what the end result is, and it's used to verify the integrity of data, but not the authenticity. We can run checksums against a piece of data, and we do this with error-correcting code, with RAM, we do it with checksums when we're sending packets on a network, and we can do the same thing here. A checksum would allow us, so to test before and after, and if those checkssums match, then we know the data has not been tampered with. We can't necessarily prove the authenticity, but we can prove that the data itself is the same. Then we have the concept of providence, which is the metadata that documents the inputs, the changes, to data and provides a historical record of the data and also its origins. In essence, it allows us to track who created the data, any changes to that data throughout its lifespan. It's a way for us to verify the integrity of data and to get a bit of a historical view on what has happened to that data since its origin.

Non-repudiation

Next we have nonrepudiation, and nonrepudiation is an accountability concept. It is an inability to refute an action or an ownership. It says the person that we think has done this or owns this or has interacted with this, they can't reasonably say no, it wasn't me. Cryptographic nonrepudiation we can think of as digital signatures. That provides the inability to refute something. If a person, as an example, has a public key/private key and then they sign something with that certificate, then that proves that they are who they are. Of course unless someone steals their certificate, then of course all bets are off. But as long as that secret is kept safe, that PKI certificate is kept safe, then that would prove that that person is who they say they are. We can also have network nonrepudiation, and center around the generation of enough data of activity so that it can't be refuted, so the action itself cannot be refuted.

On-prem vs. Cloud Challenges and to Audit

Let's talk about some of the on-prem versus cloud challenges. We have three things to cover. We have the -to-audit clauses, we have regulatory and jurisdictional issues, and then data breach notification laws. Auditors will typically routinely access on-prem data centers to perform audits as needed. It can be regulatory or compliance mandates. It can be investigations of breaches. It can be contractual, annual, or biannual audits. You could have customers and your customers need some type of certification or understanding that you are providing security controls and that you're doing things effectively, best practices. If that's the case, you want your customers to be able to have documentation and proof that these things exist. But having things in the cloud can pose unique challenges to auditing, because cloud providers typically don't allow auditors in, just because of their sheer size. Cloud providers typically have thousands or potentially tens of thousands of clients or tenants, and if those tenants were routinely allowing auditors or having auditors come in to audit their infrastructure, it would get very unruly, very quickly, and the cloud provider wouldn't be able to get anything done, like business-as-usual, day-to-day work, because they'd have auditors in there, inspecting things 24/7, 365. There are ways around that, though, and you can still prove that you are, in fact, following best practices and having your security controls in place. Let's say, for instance, we have a data center or a cloud provider, a co-location facility, and in there, we have a number of tenants who have IaaS and SaaS, infrastructure as a service, software as a service, virtualization equipment. Well, we need to be able to provide a way to have those things audited and show definitively that we're following best practices, our security controls are in place. There are two organizations that I just want to call to your attention. One is SSAE 18, and that stands for the Statement on Standards for Attestation Engagements, number 18, and then internationally, we have ISAE 3402, that provides similar guidance. Those certification bodies have three different types of reporting. We have SOC 1, SOC 2, and SOC 3, and

SOC stands for Service Organization Control, or SOC reports? There are three different types: SOC 1, 2, and 3. SOC 1 deals with financial reporting controls, SOC 2 deals with security controls, and then SOC 3 is publicly accessible. What these do is they ensure that data centers, channel partners, and vendors, utilize the same security controls as the data center or hosting provider? And all of these things are in place. Then there are two different types. Within SOC 1 and SOC 2, there are two different types, which we'll talk about here. Type 1 is an attestation of controls at a service organization, at a specific point in time. An auditor will give their opinion and say, they have these controls in place, but they don't verify or validate their effectiveness; they don't test them. It's a point in time. Type 2 reports is an attestation of controls at a service organization over a minimum six-month period, so it's a much more involved type of report, but they go through and not just validate that the controls were there, but they test them, and make sure that they're workable, they're effective, and they do what they say they're going to do. Two types of reports; 1 is easier to get or get certified against; Type 2 is more comprehensive, as you may guess, but once you're certified, your clients, customers have a strong understanding of what controls are in place and that they're effective. Then the SOC 3 type of report, those types of reports have the basic information, but the details, the under-the-hood type of things, are stripped away, and that's made publicly accessible, so that anyone can look and see what controls are there or what types of controls are there, but not the details, not the inner workings.

Chapter 23 Jurisdictional Issues & Data Breach Notification Laws

As a business, once you start to put things into the cloud you run into some potential issues, not necessarily every time, but some things to definitely think about. Data sovereignty and accessing that data, who owns or maintains or has jurisdiction over that data, can vary from country to country. Some countries are stricter, they have stricter laws, while others are less restrictive. It just depends upon where that data is stored. That can impact the ability to access the data, to audit data. So, data sovereignty, that states that the legal restrictions of any jurisdiction where data is collected, stored, or processed can apply. Depending upon where your information is stored, what region, what part of the world, different jurisdictional laws can apply. It's important that you know that. As an example, let's say we have a global business. We're doing business all over the world. We have customers all over the world. We may have a data center in one part of the world, maybe another data center somewhere else, and then another data center somewhere else. If we're a cloud provider or we're using a cloud provider, it's important to understand that cloud providers typically will have data centers all over the world. They do that purposely, so they can disperse that infrastructure globally, provide for geo redundancy and failover. Data can potentially be copied, stored, or processed anywhere globally. SoData is often copied between data centers in different regions. ? They might stay within a specific country, but it's copied within regions to make sure you have that redundancy, high availability. But it could potentially be copied somewhere else. ? Be sure to know where your data's stored. If it's copied between regions or between geo dispersed regions outside or into other countries, make sure you're aware of the applicable laws that may be in play. Also, if you have customers in other countries then data might be stored local to that region. An investigation or a breach or some type of audit could be impacted by that specific country's data privacy laws, data sovereignty laws.

Data Breach Notification Laws

They were first enacted in 2002, roughly almost 20 years ago. All 50 states have data breach notification laws, although it took probably 15-18 years to get all 50 states on board. But individuals and companies affected by a data breach must notify their customers. That's the general gist of the laws. Then they must also take specific steps to remediate any deficiencies. If a breach occurs and we identify why that happened, the companies must make sure that they're doing the proper steps to remediate and get rid of those issues, fill those gaps and make sure it doesn't happen again. Something also worth noting is that there's no federal data breach notification law currently. There are certain regulatory mandates that have certain industries disclose breaches, but not across the board of federal notification law. There are also data breach notification laws in other countries, so it's not just a US thing. Australia, China, the EU, Japan, New Zealand, etc., they are examples of other countries that have similar data breach notification laws. Then there are certain regulations that can affect customers or companies globally like GDPR, California's CCPA, there are a number of other ones in other countries as well. But just understand that just because you reside in a specific location, if you do business globally or if you utilize a cloud provider you may potentially be subject to other countries' laws, data sovereignty laws, or to privacy, to notification laws. It's very important that you understand all the nuances, and then wherever that data resides, if it's processed, collected, stored, there are applicable laws that may impact how you do business, depending upon where it's located. In this chapter we talked about documentation and evidence, the acquisition of that evidence, how to collect it, the order of volatility, where you should start collecting data first. We talked about the integrity of data and how we need to ensure that it hasn't been tampered with, and we can prove that. We talked about preservation and e-discovery, along with data recovery, non-repudiation, being able to certify or attest that something is what they say it is or some action was performed as we suspect it was performed. We talked about strategic intelligence and counterintelligence and then some nuances and challenges on-prem versus the cloud when it comes to storage of data, data acquisition, data sovereignty.

Conclusion

Congratulations on completing this book! I am sure you have plenty on your belt, but please don't forget to leave an honest review. Furthermore, if you think this information was helpful to you, please share anyone who you think would be interested of IT as well.

About Richie Miller

Richie Miller has always loved teaching people Technology. He graduated with a degree in radio production with a minor in theatre in order to be a better communicator. While teaching at the Miami Radio and Television Broadcasting Academy, Richie was able to do voiceover work at a technical training company specializing in live online classes in Microsoft, Cisco, and CompTia technologies. Over the years, he became one of the top virtual instructors at several training companies, while also speaking at many tech and training conferences. Richie specializes in Project Management and ITIL these days, while also doing his best to be a good husband and father.